Shining Mandala

Copyright: Published in the United States by Scott McDowell
Published January 2017
ISBN-13: 978-1542650755
ISBN-10: 1542650755

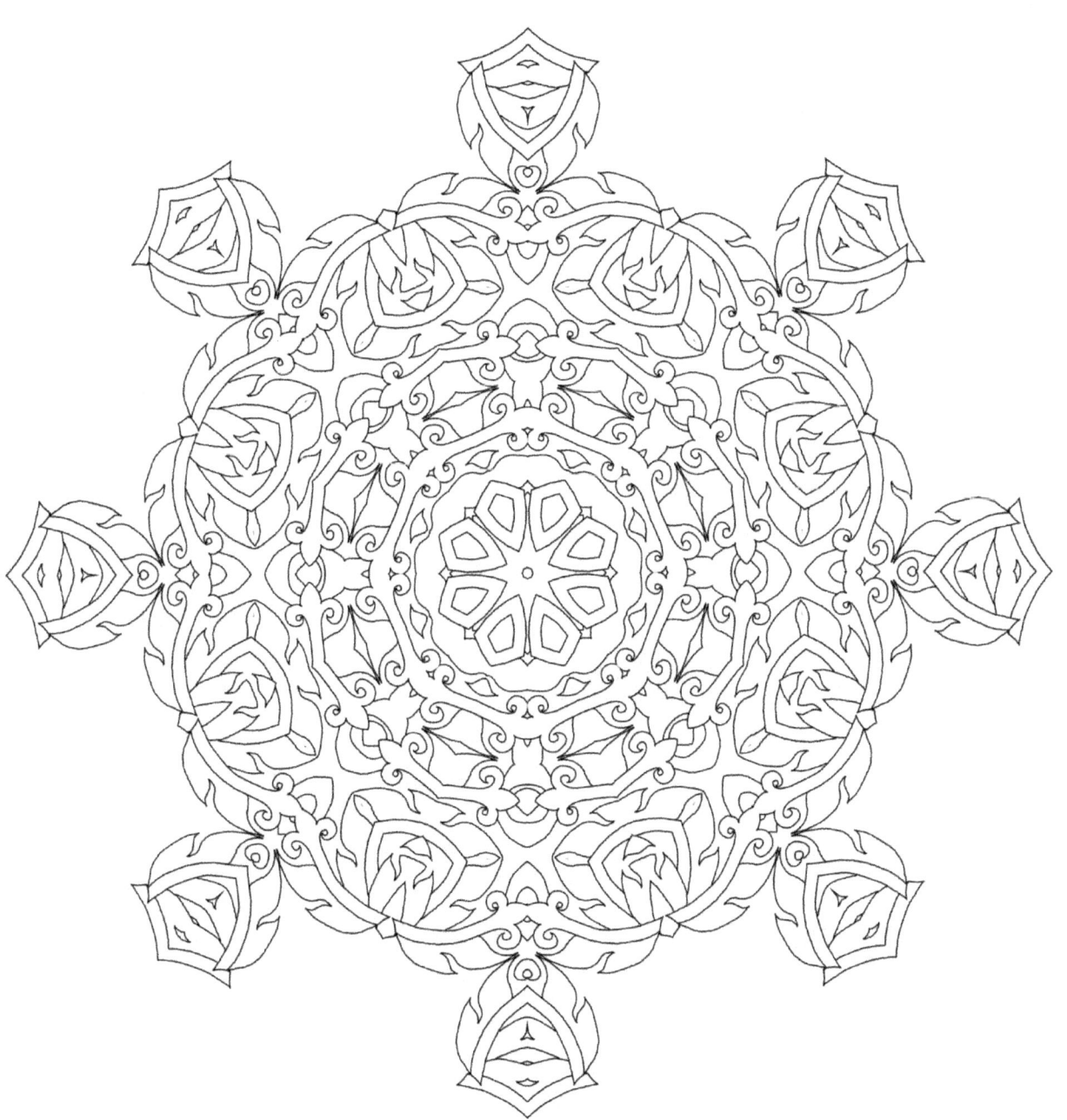

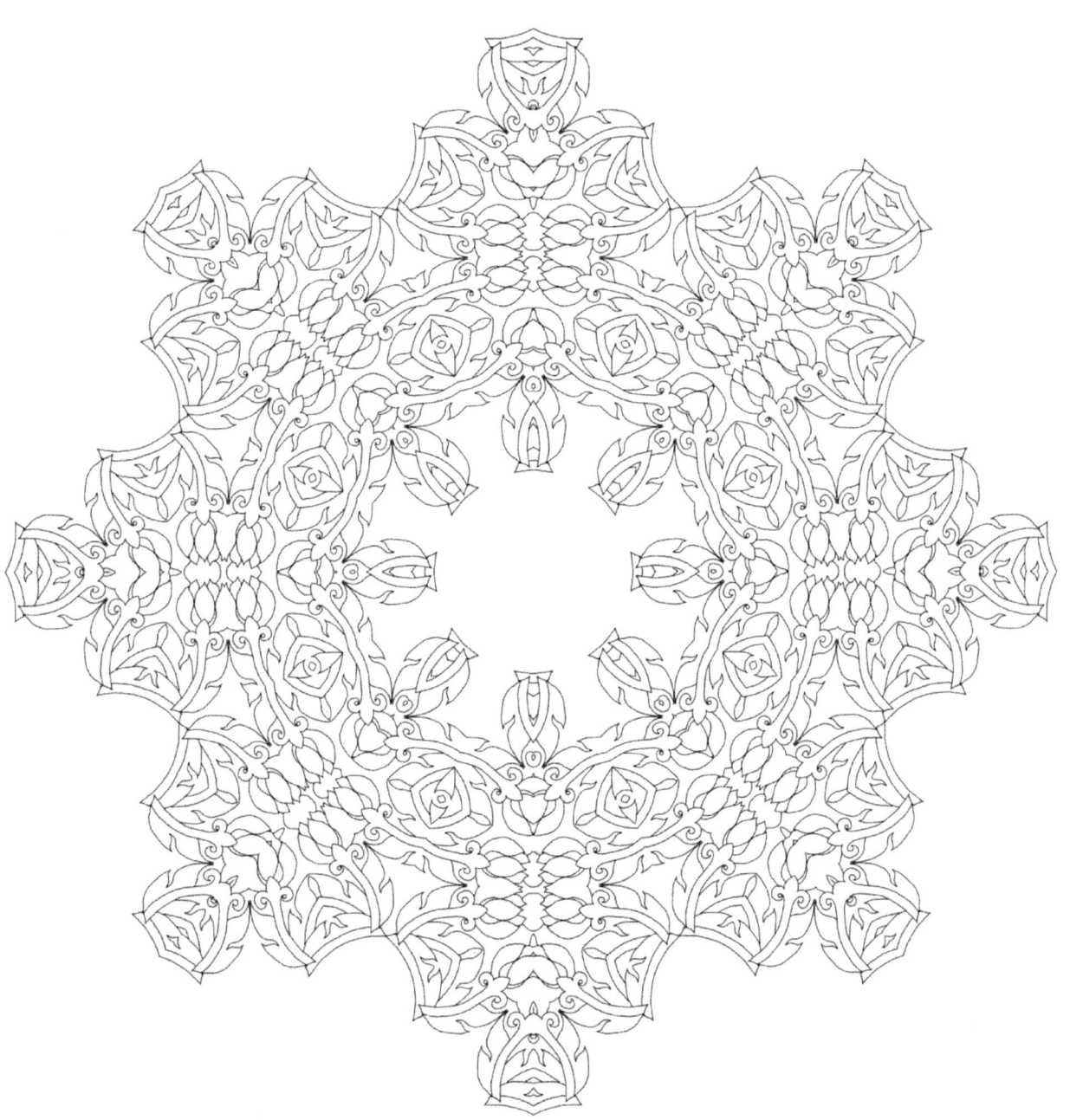

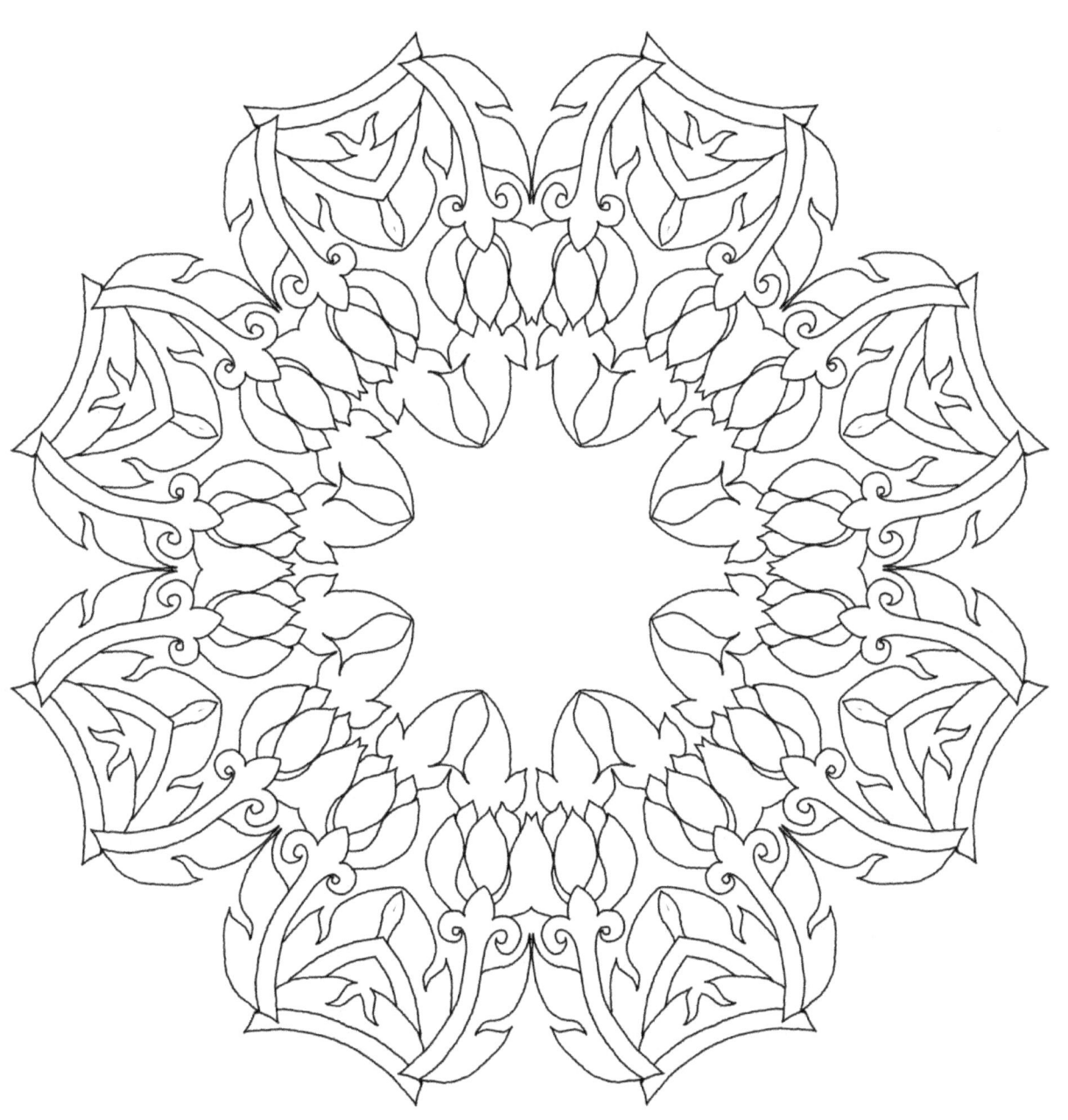

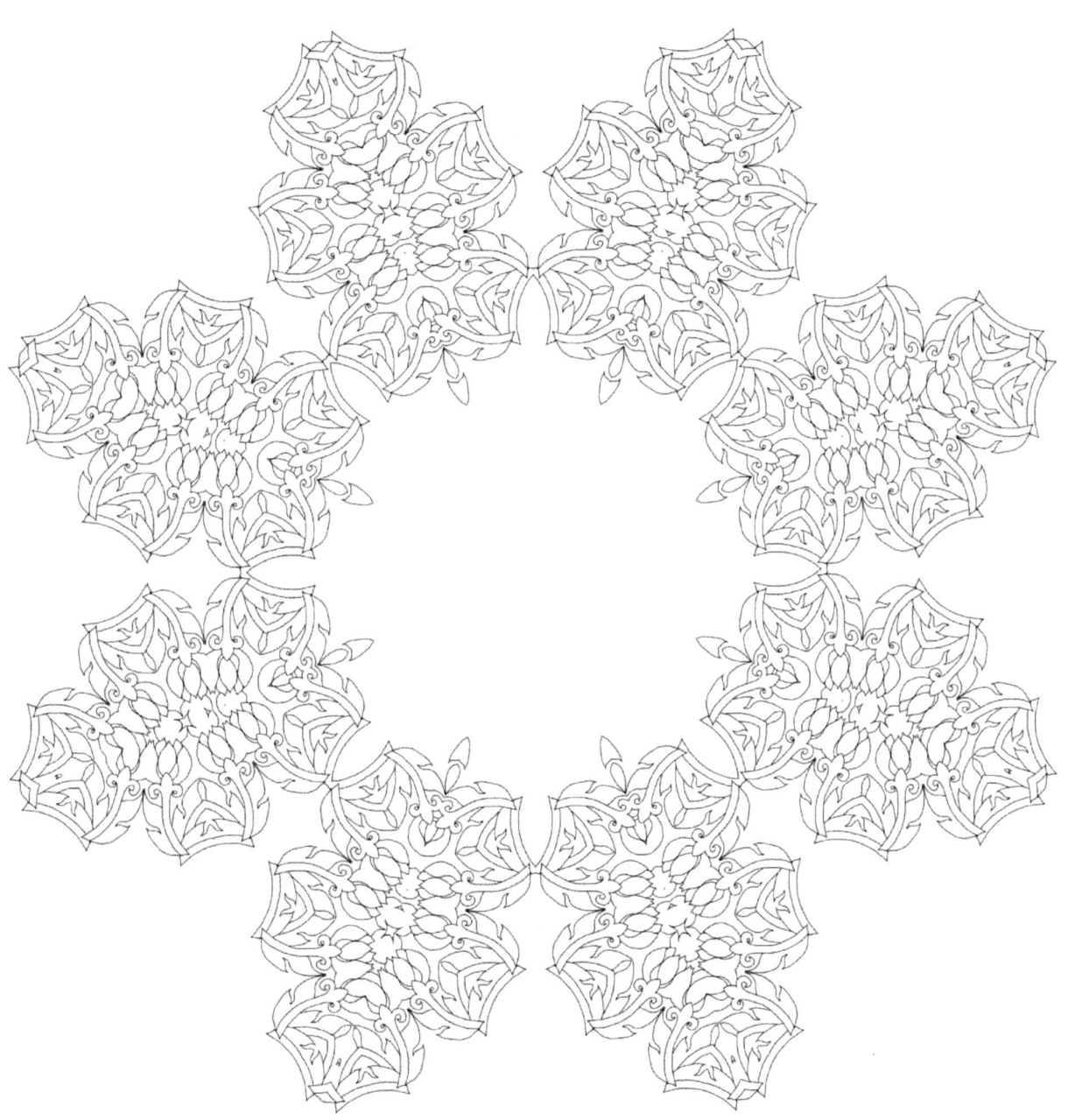

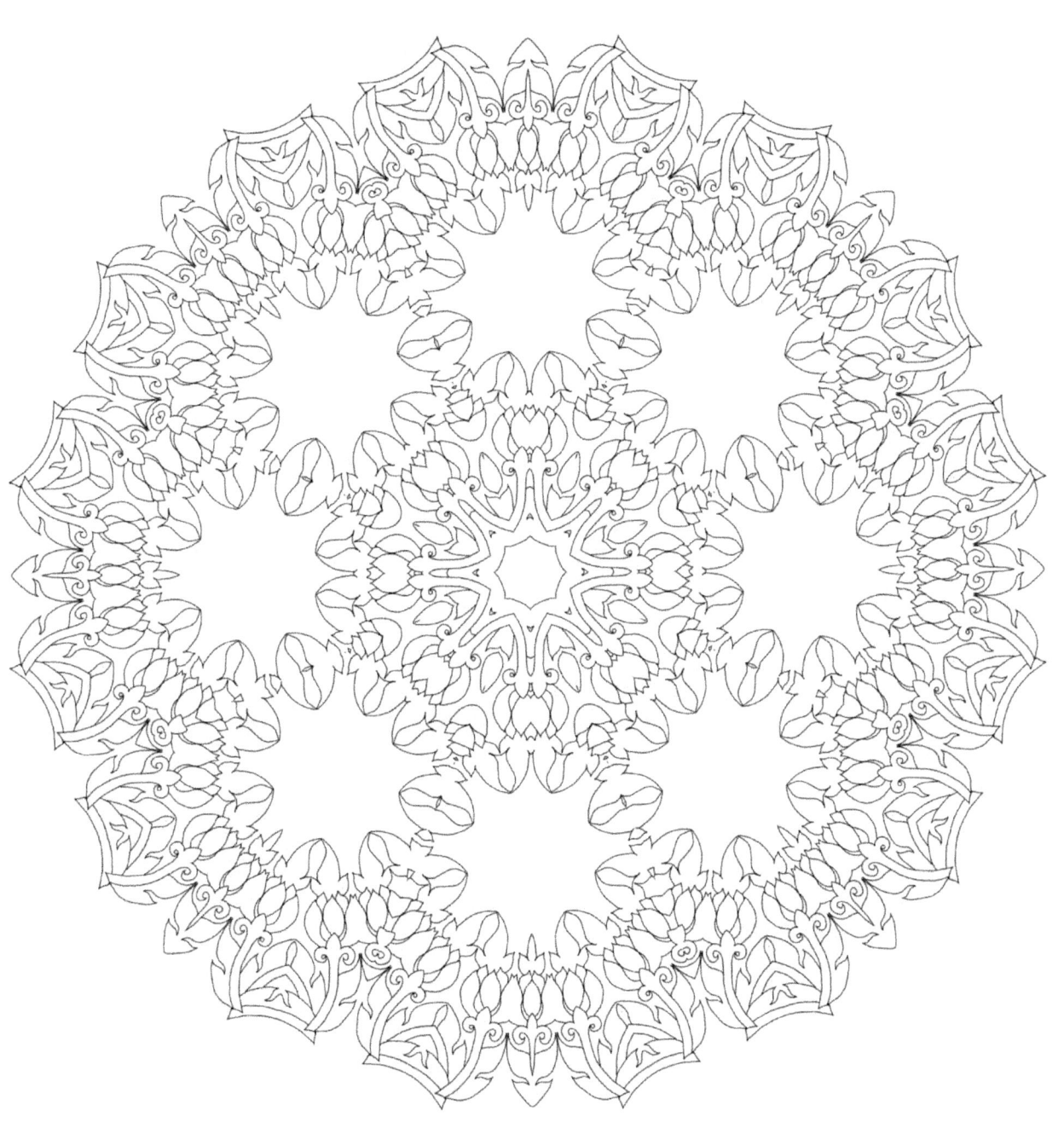

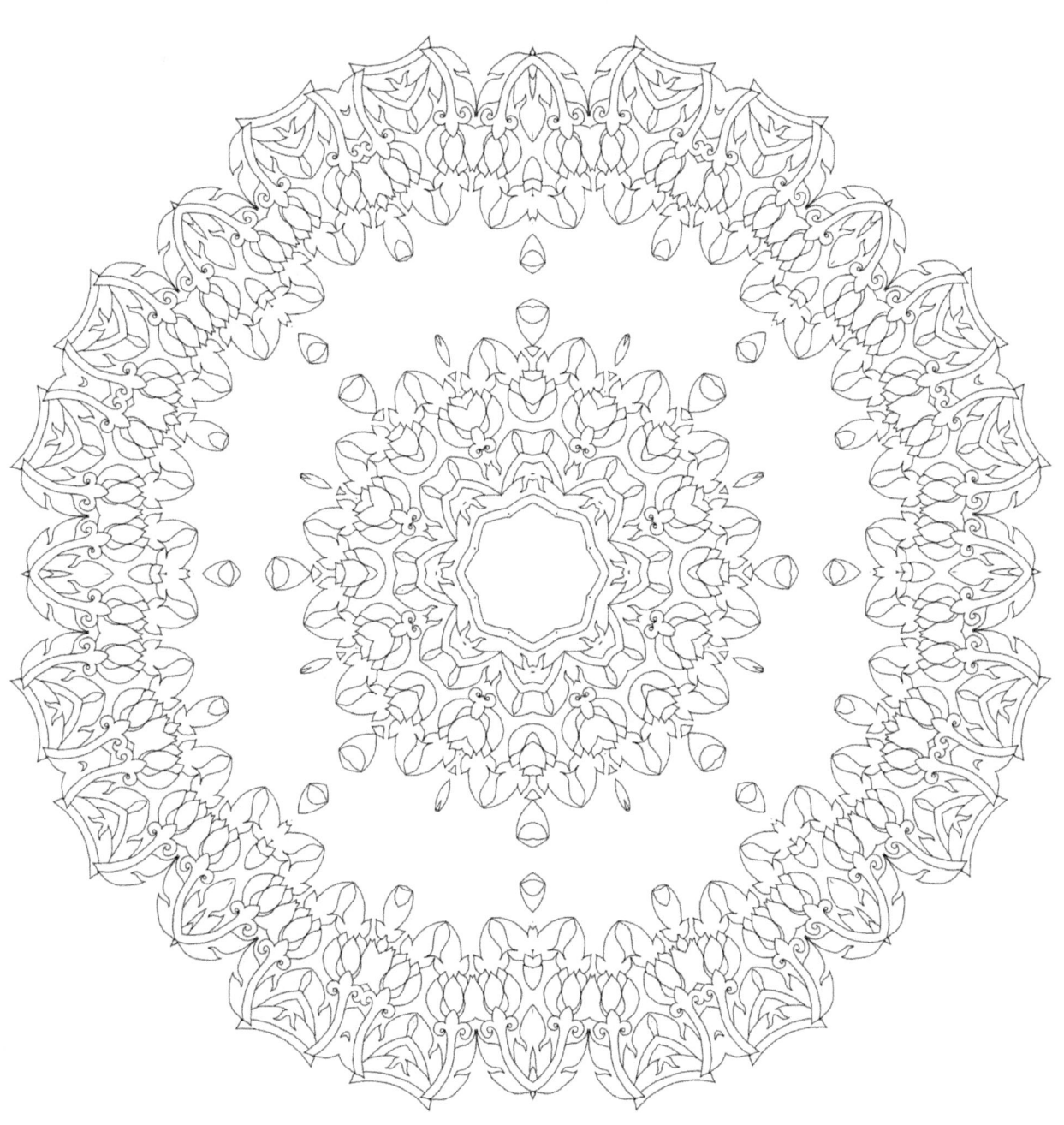

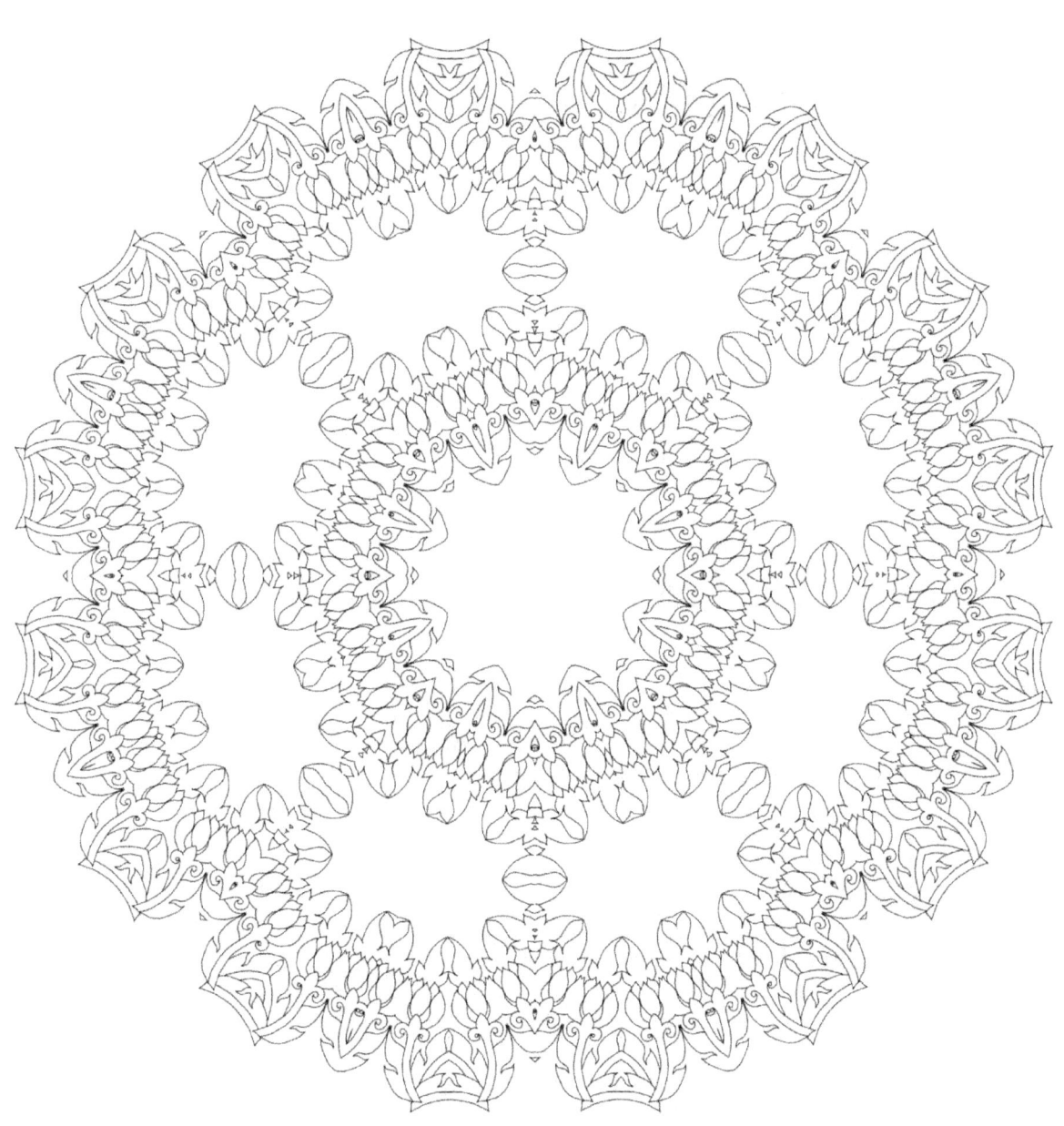

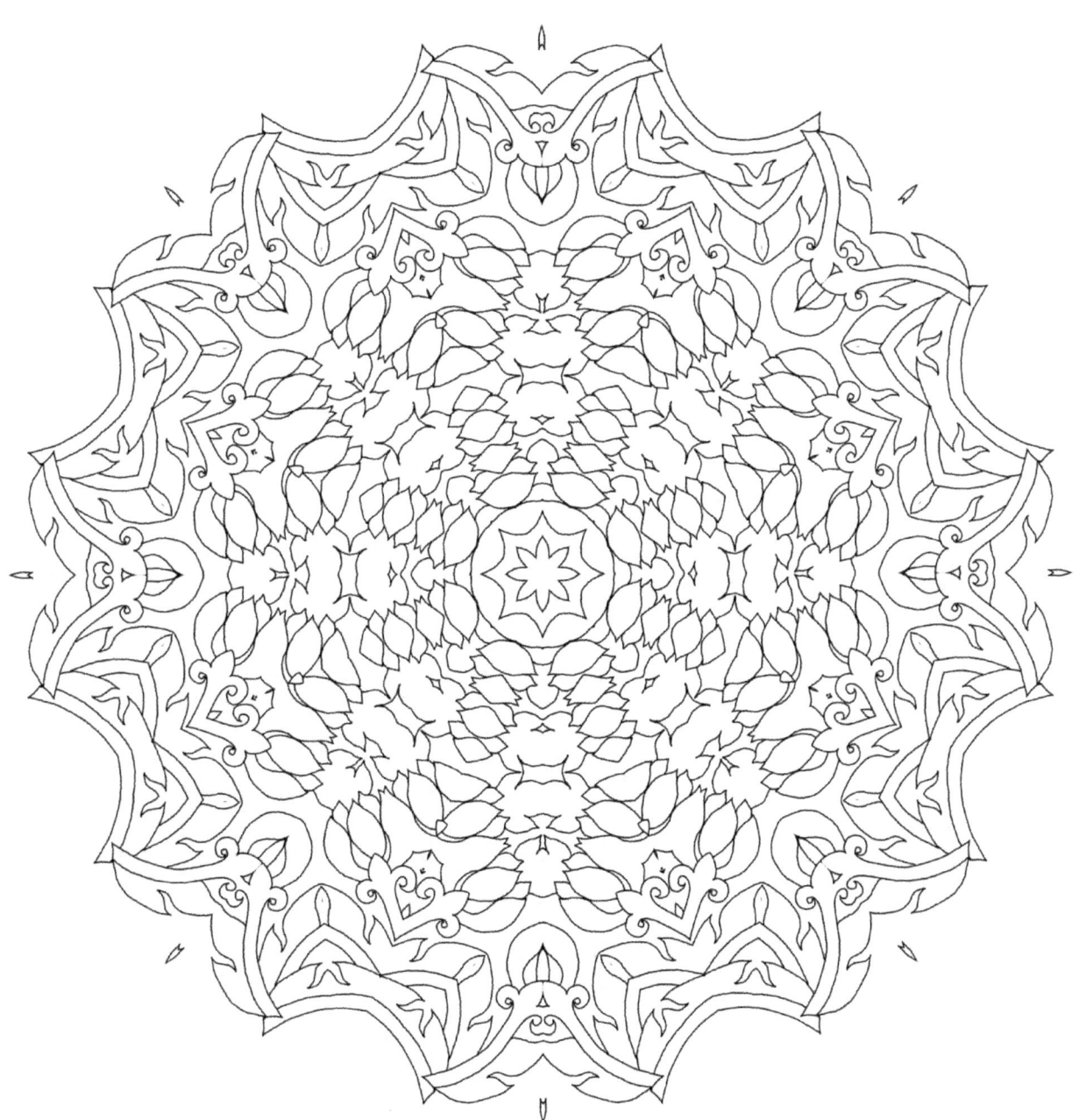

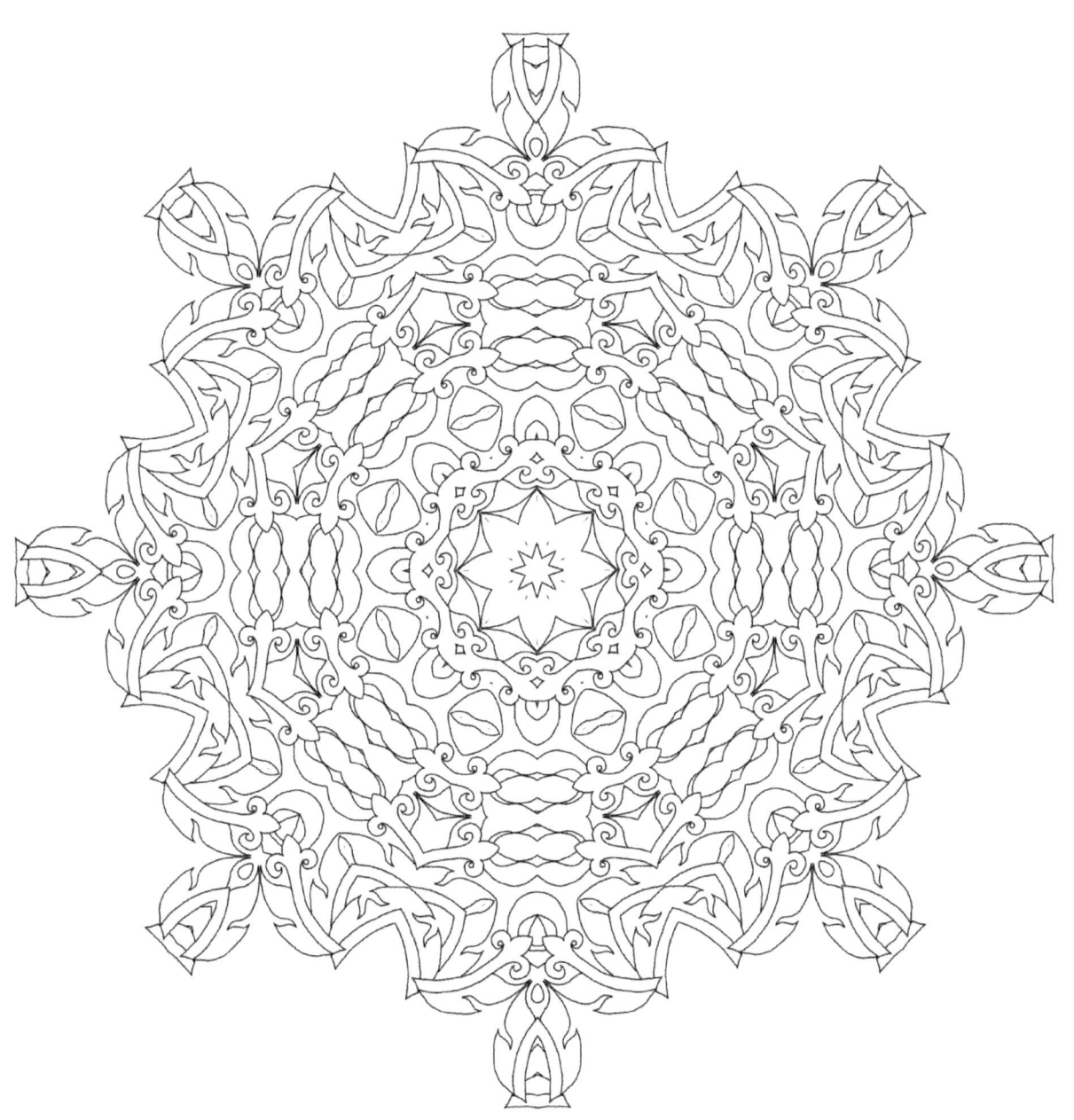

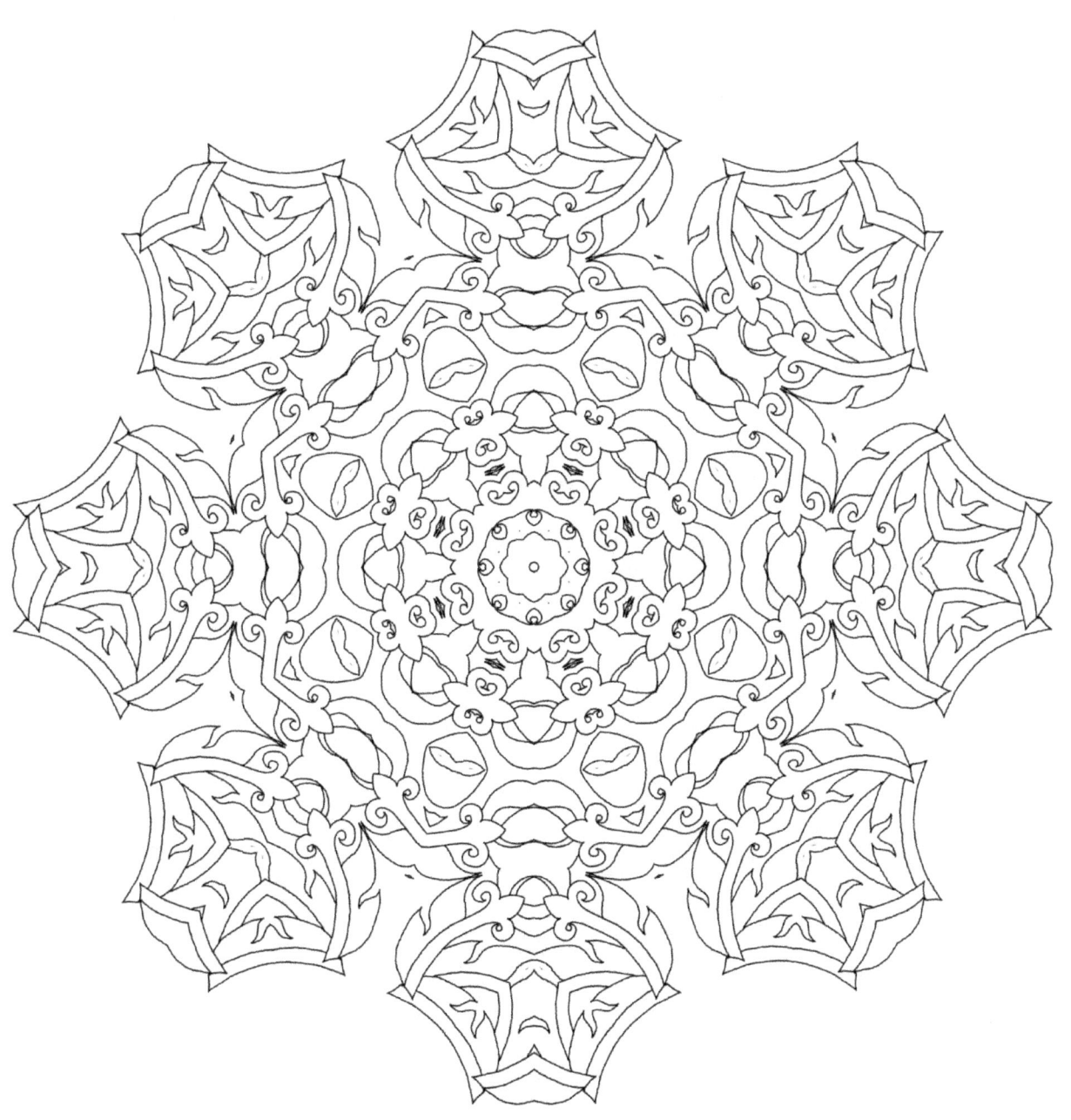

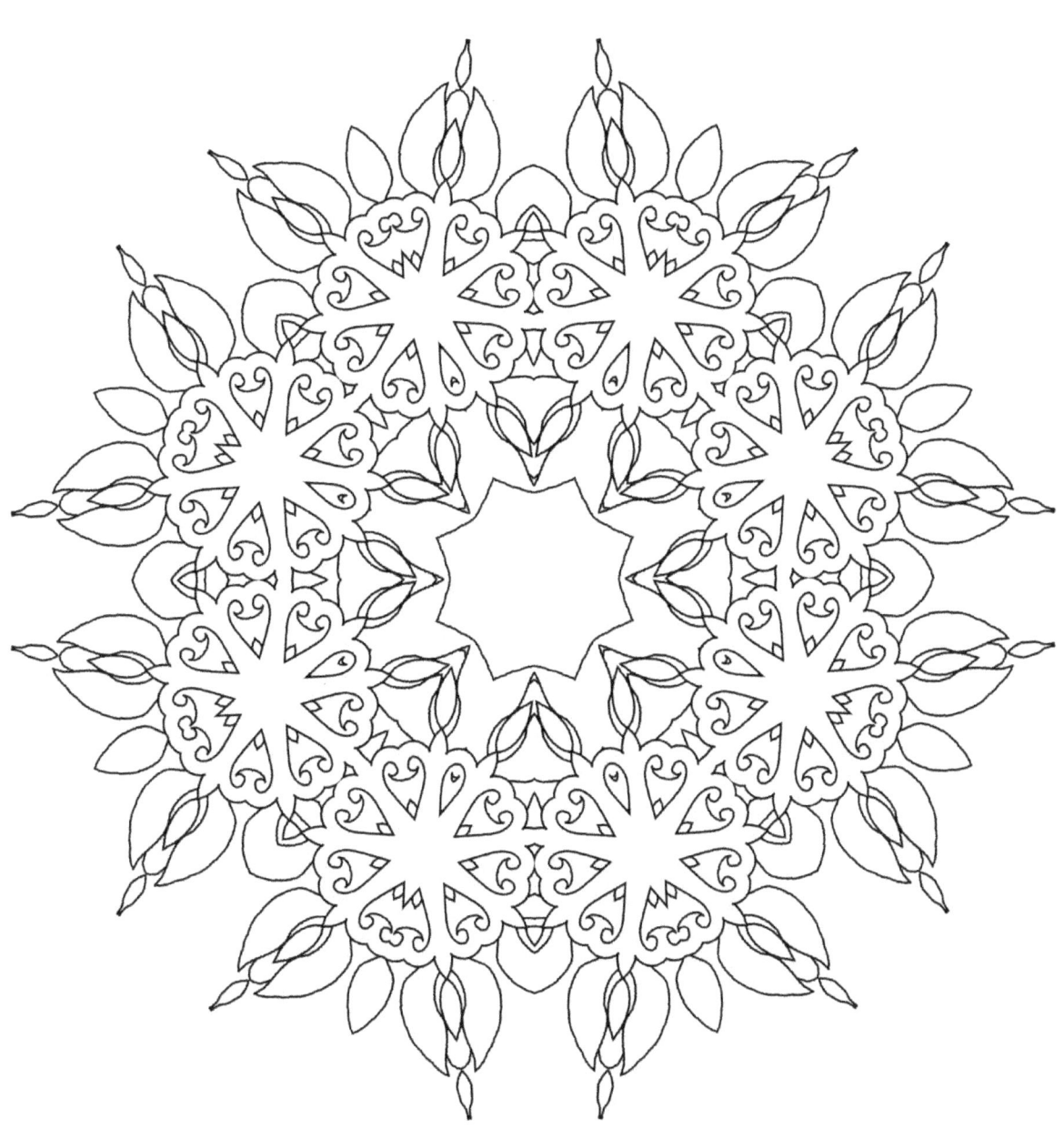

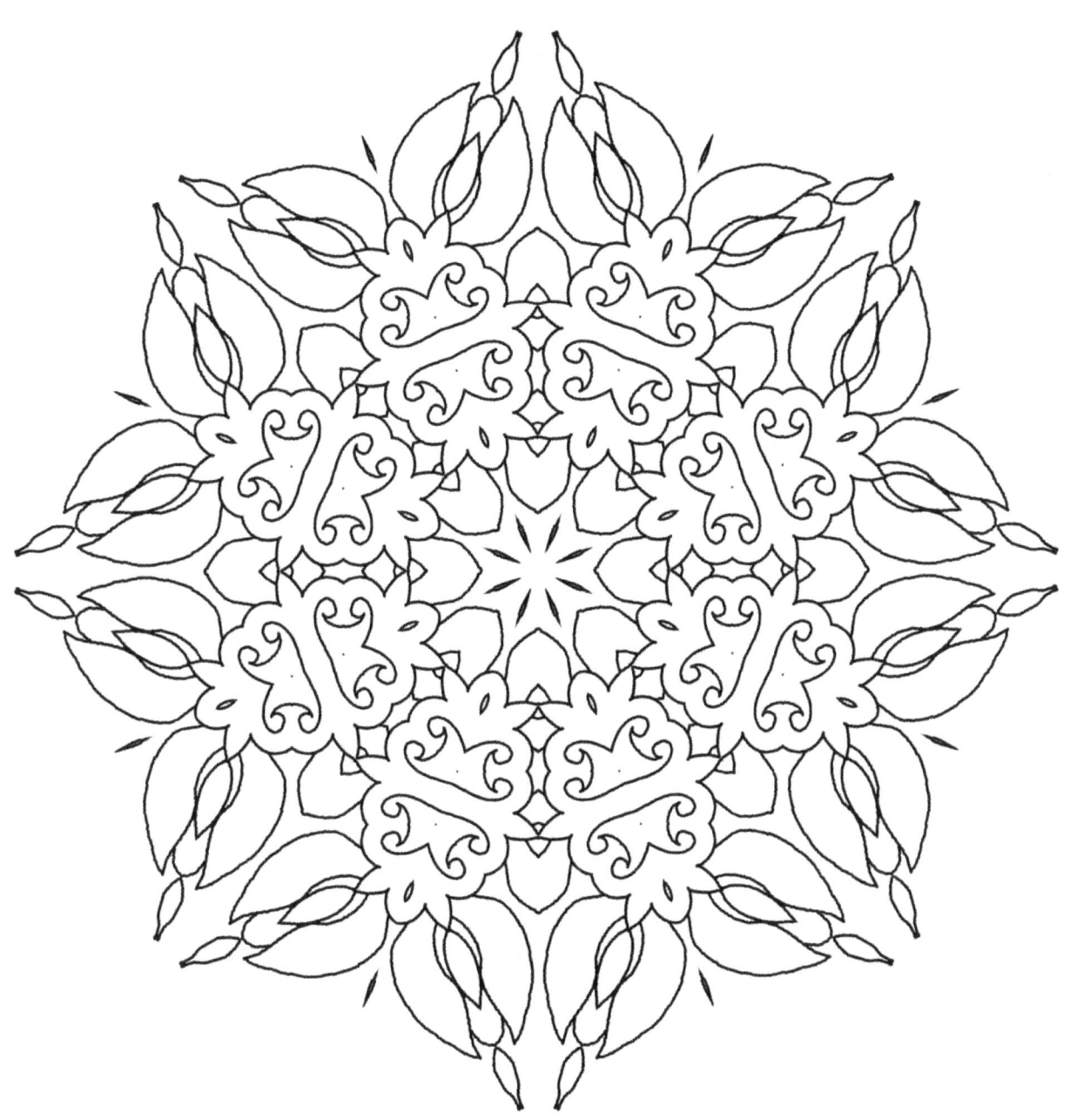

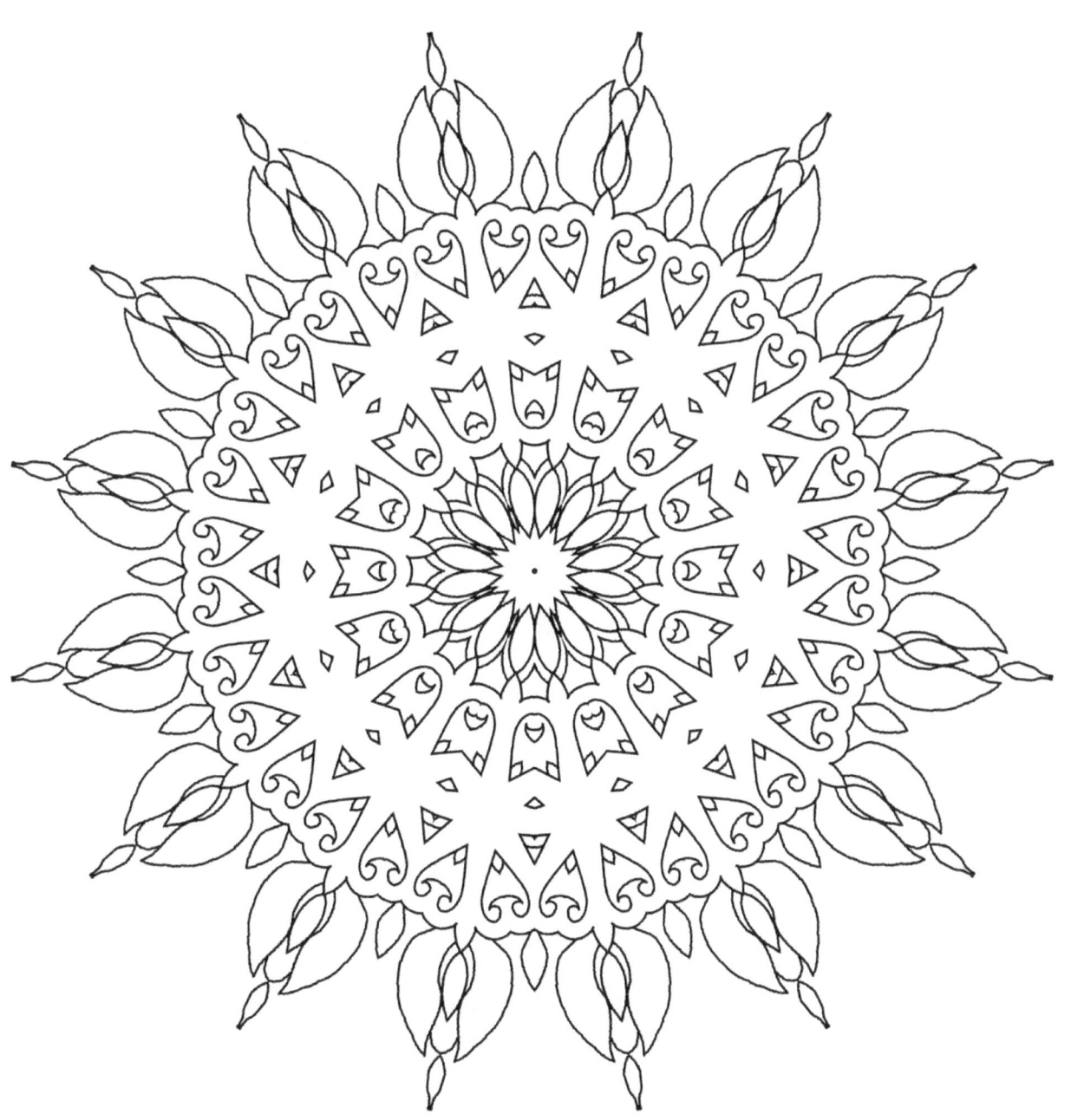

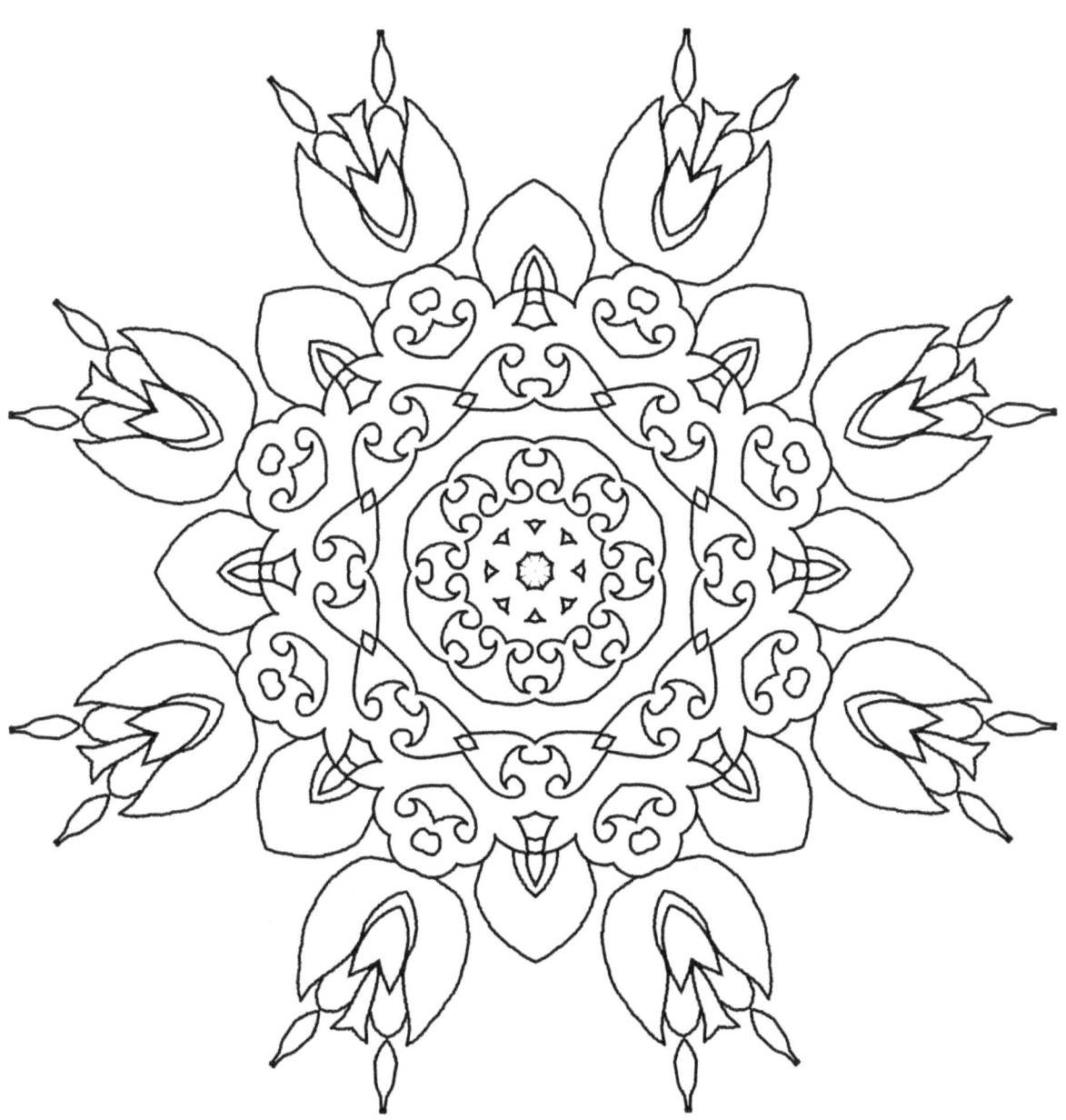

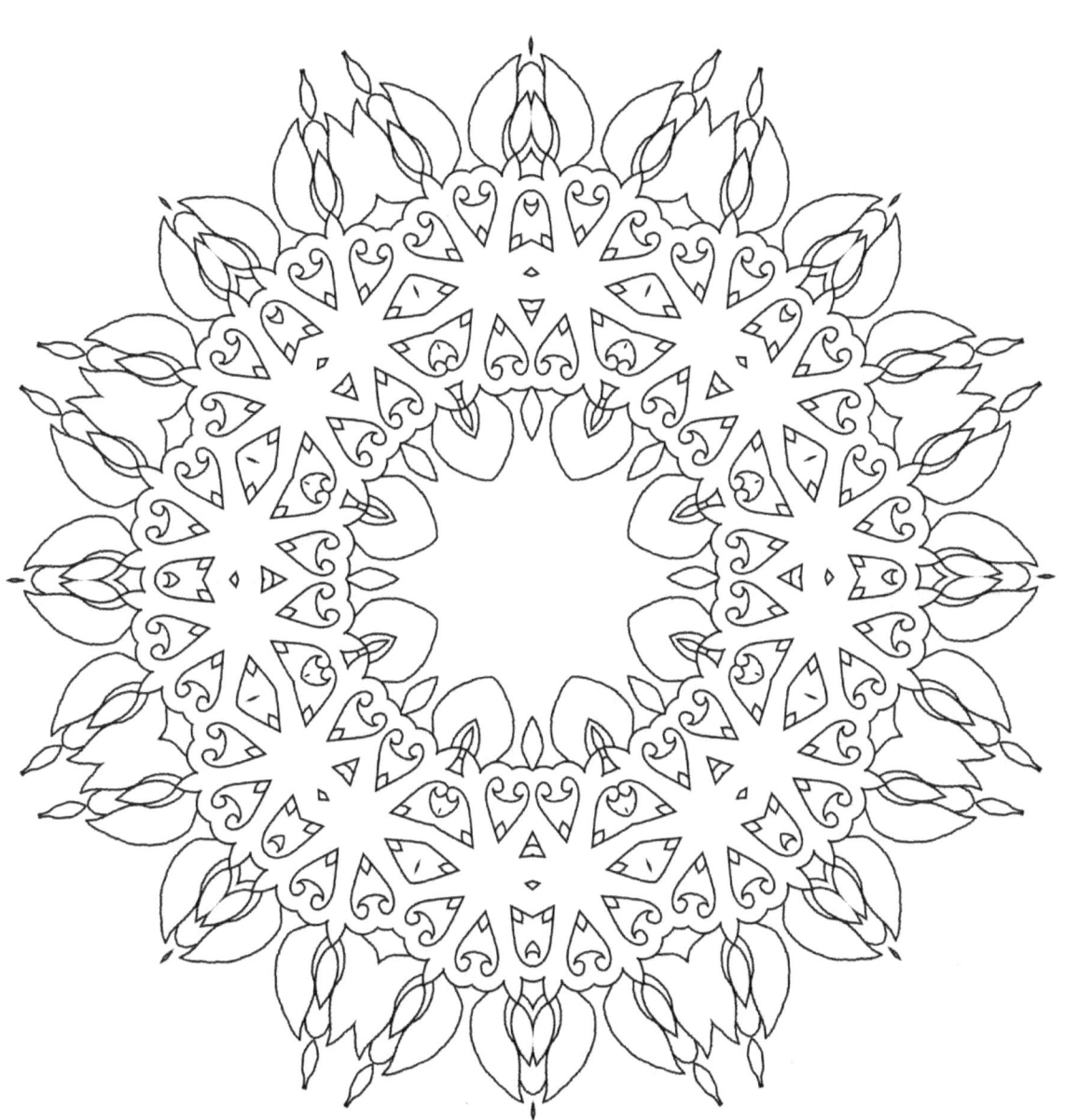

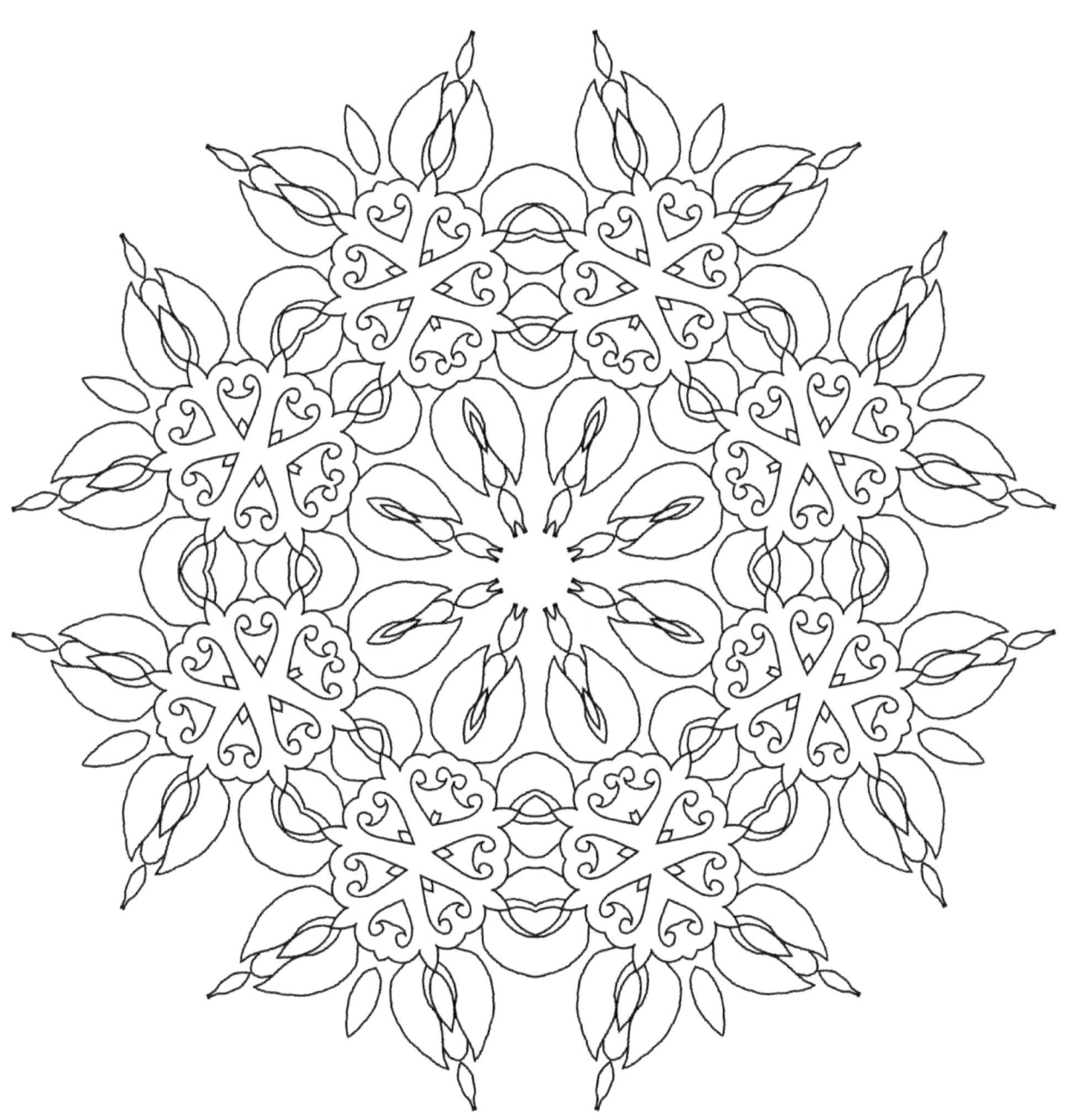

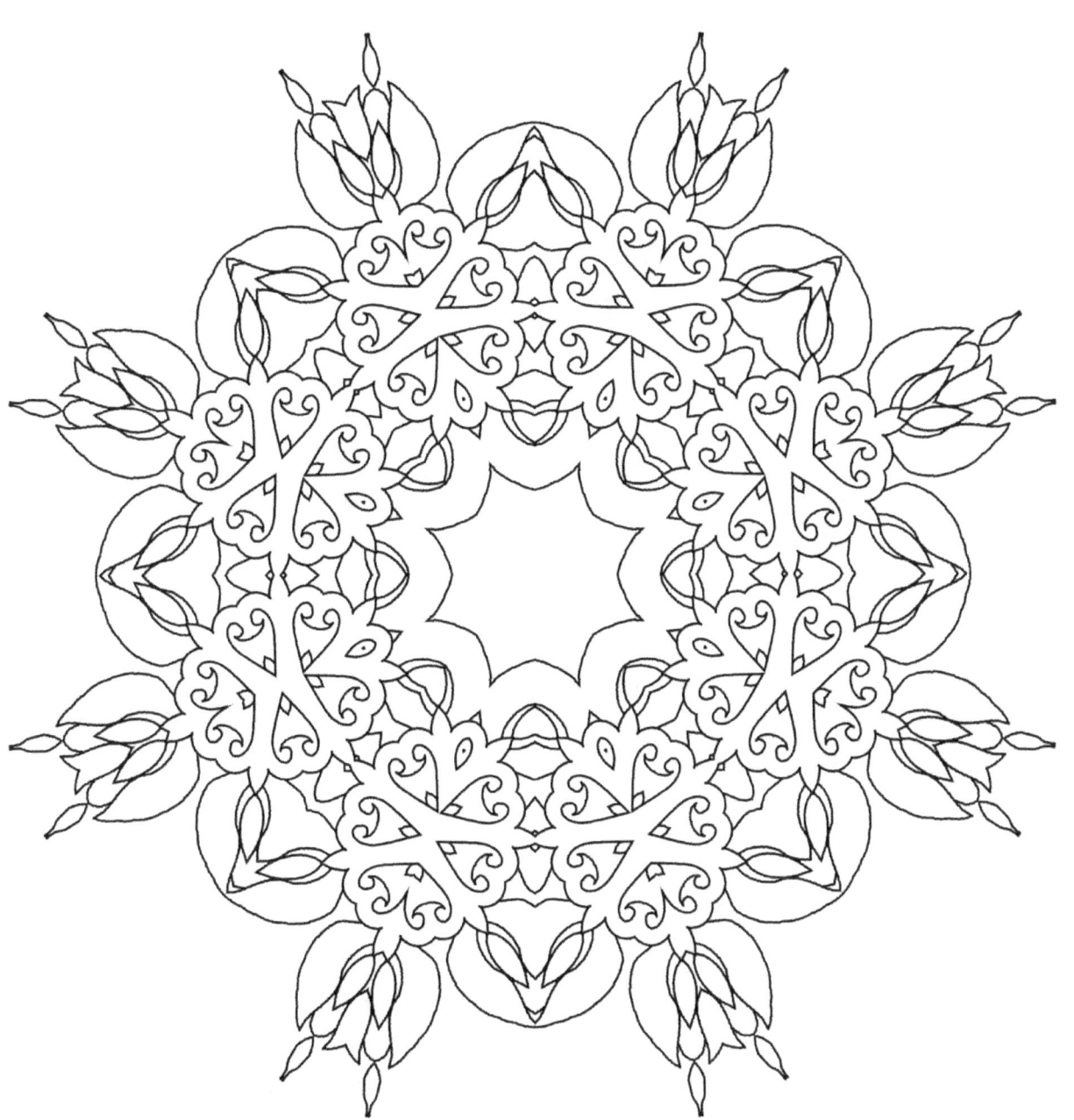

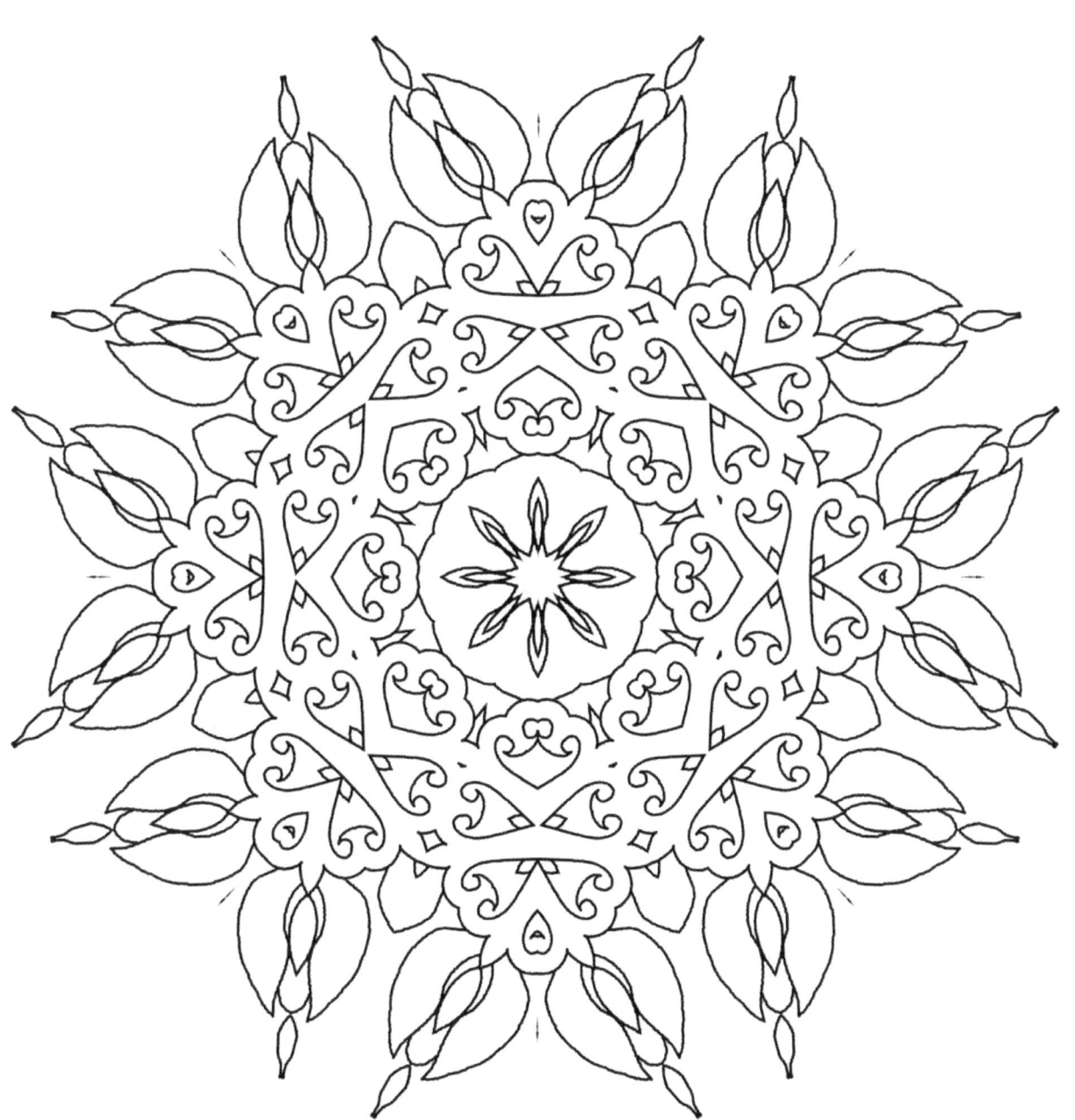

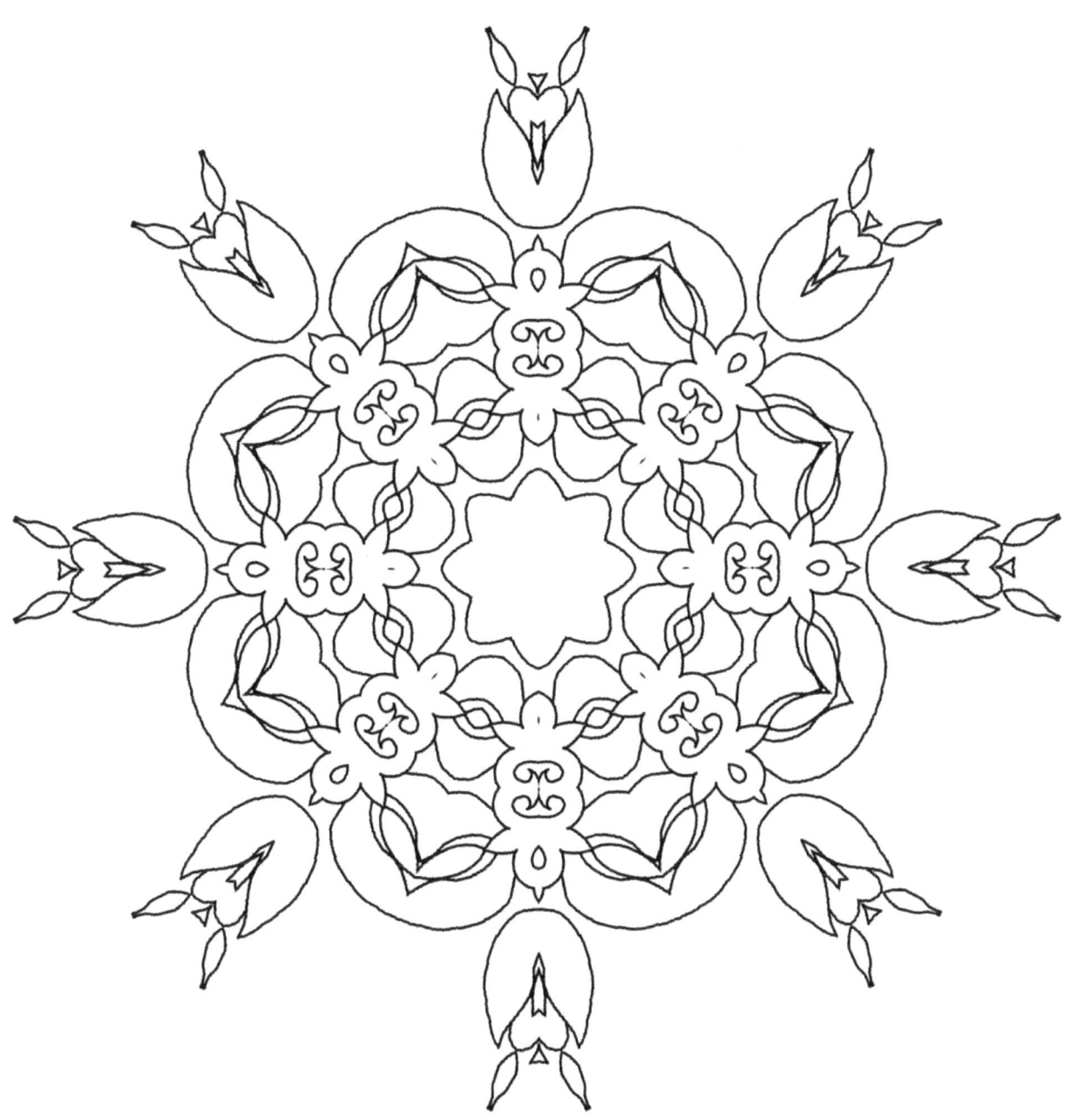

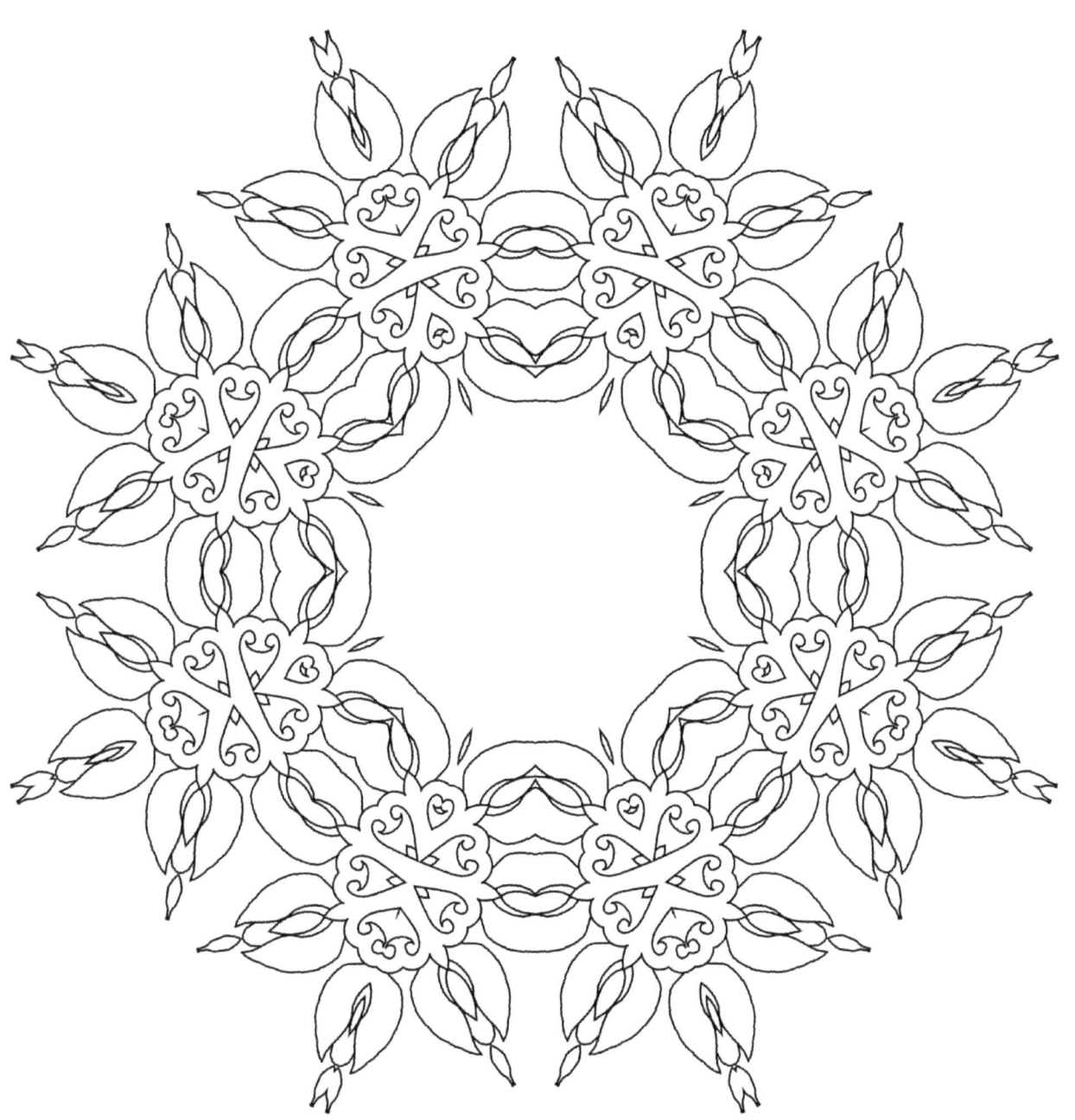

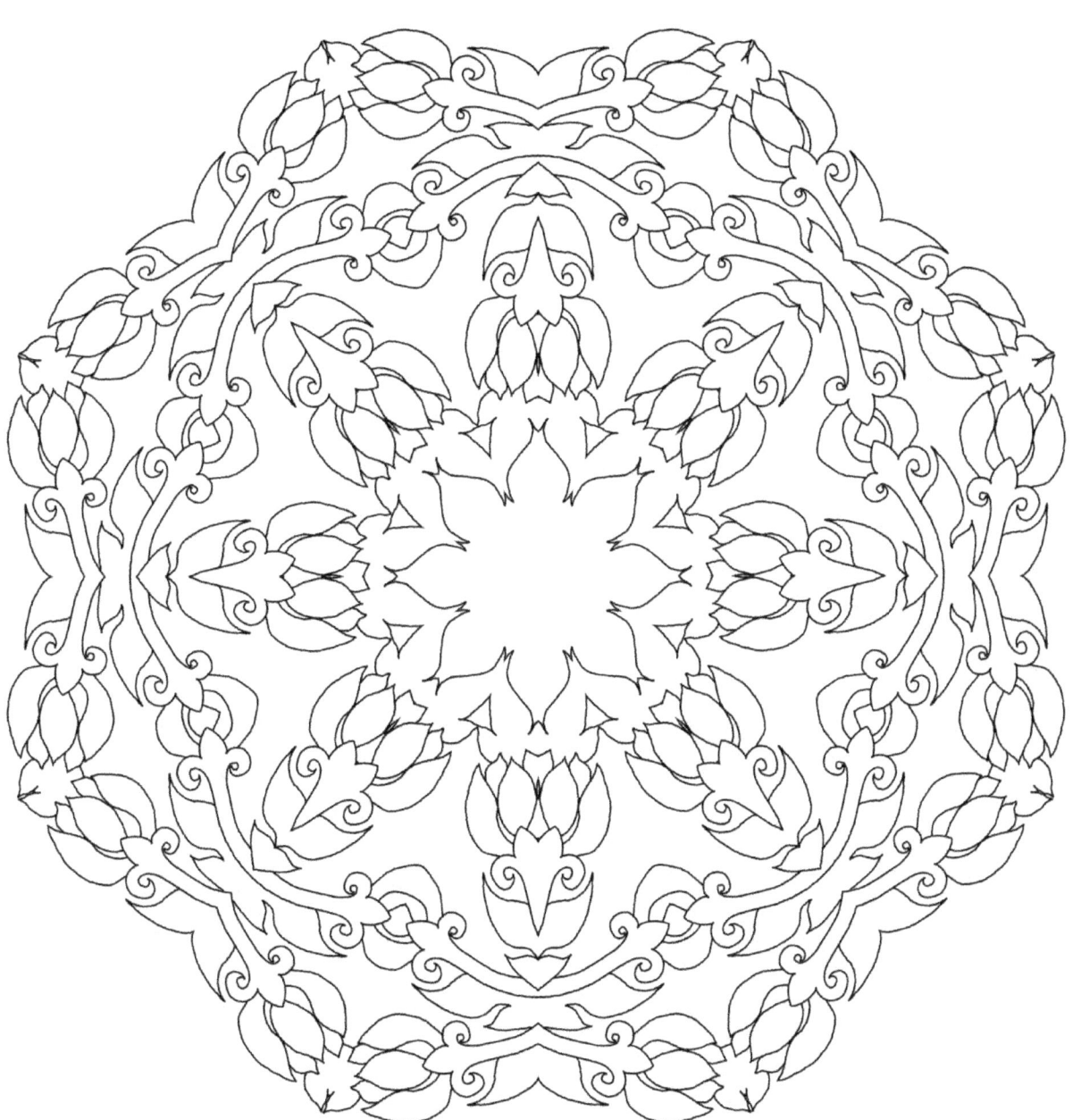

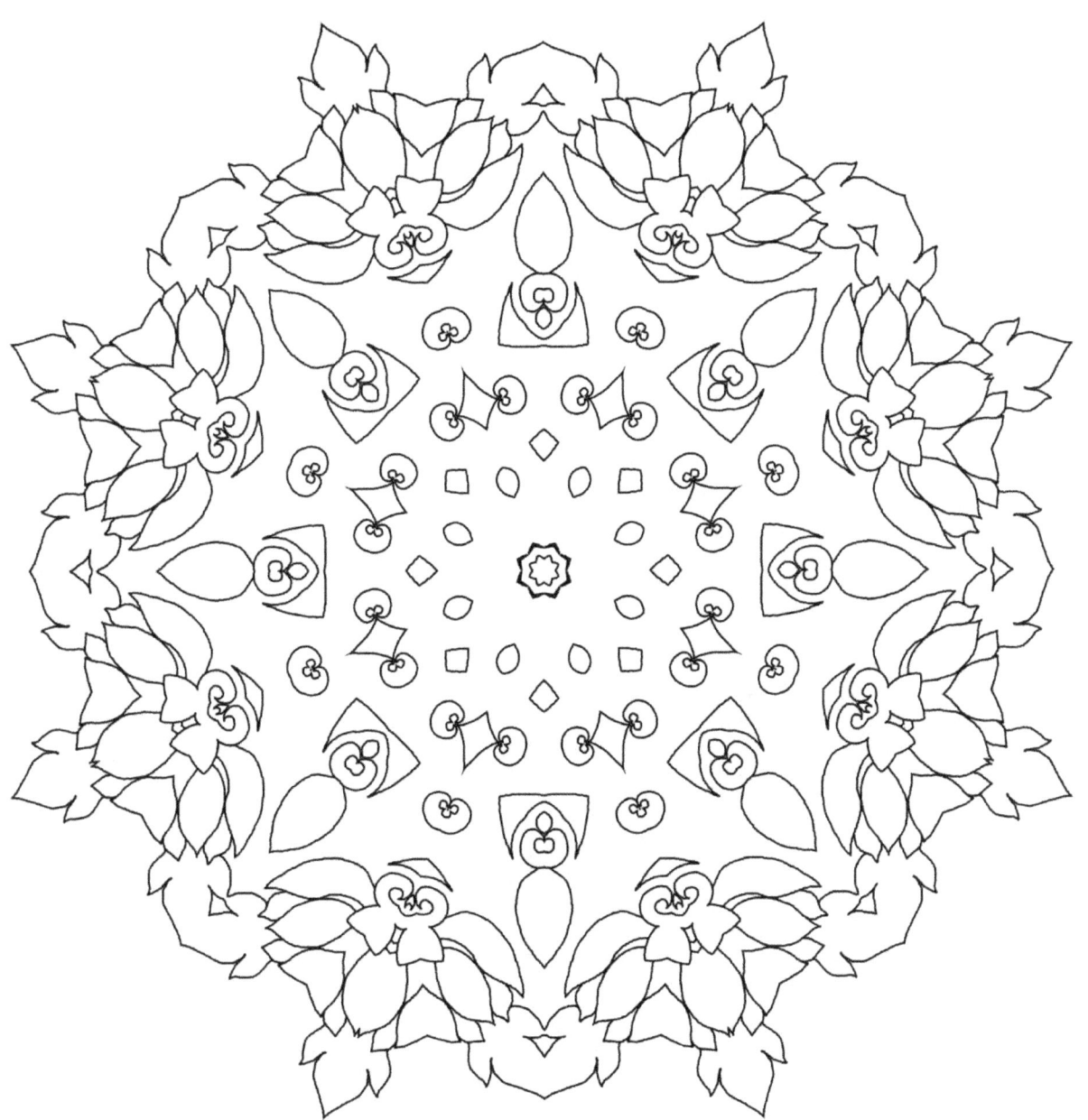

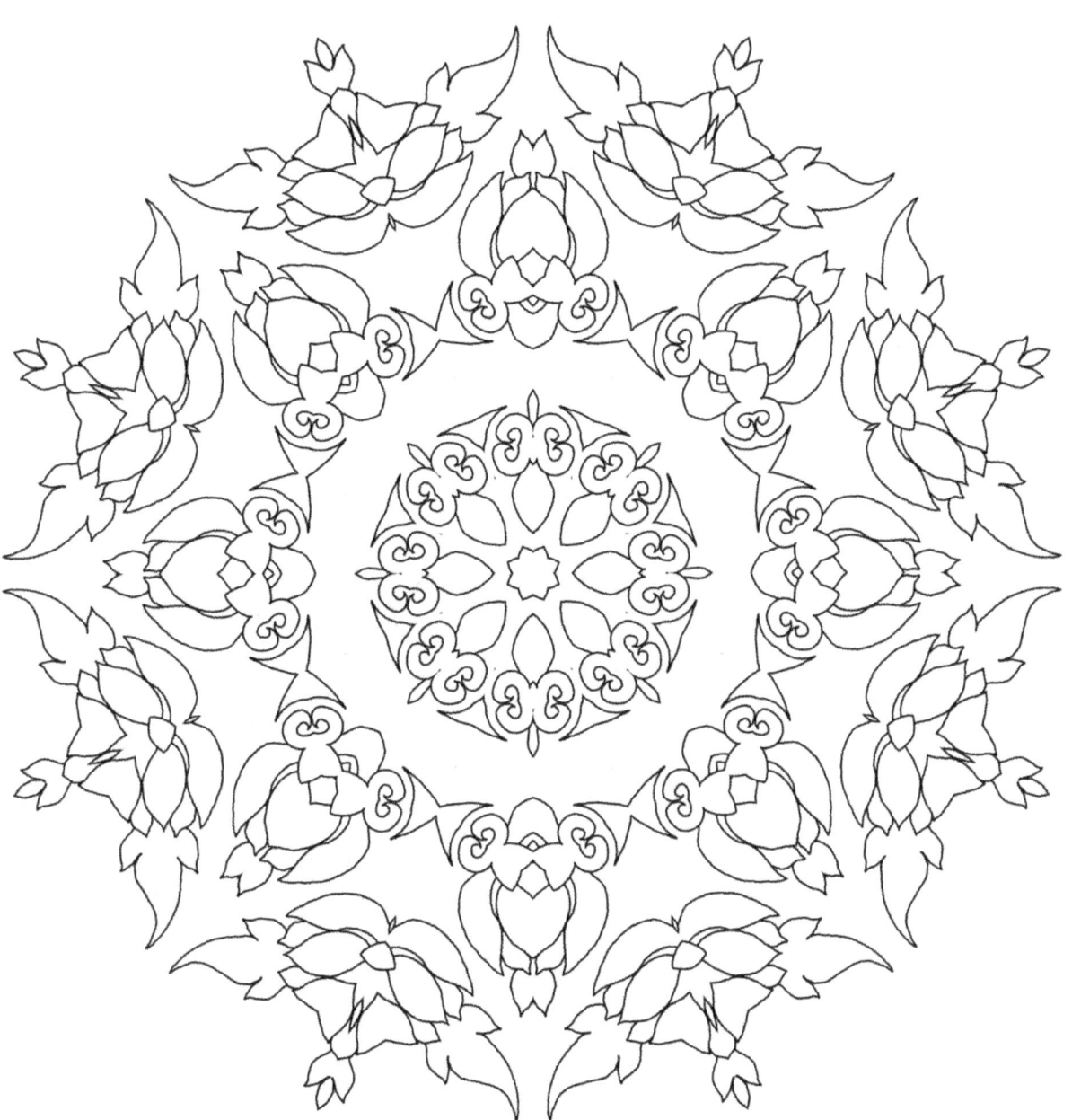

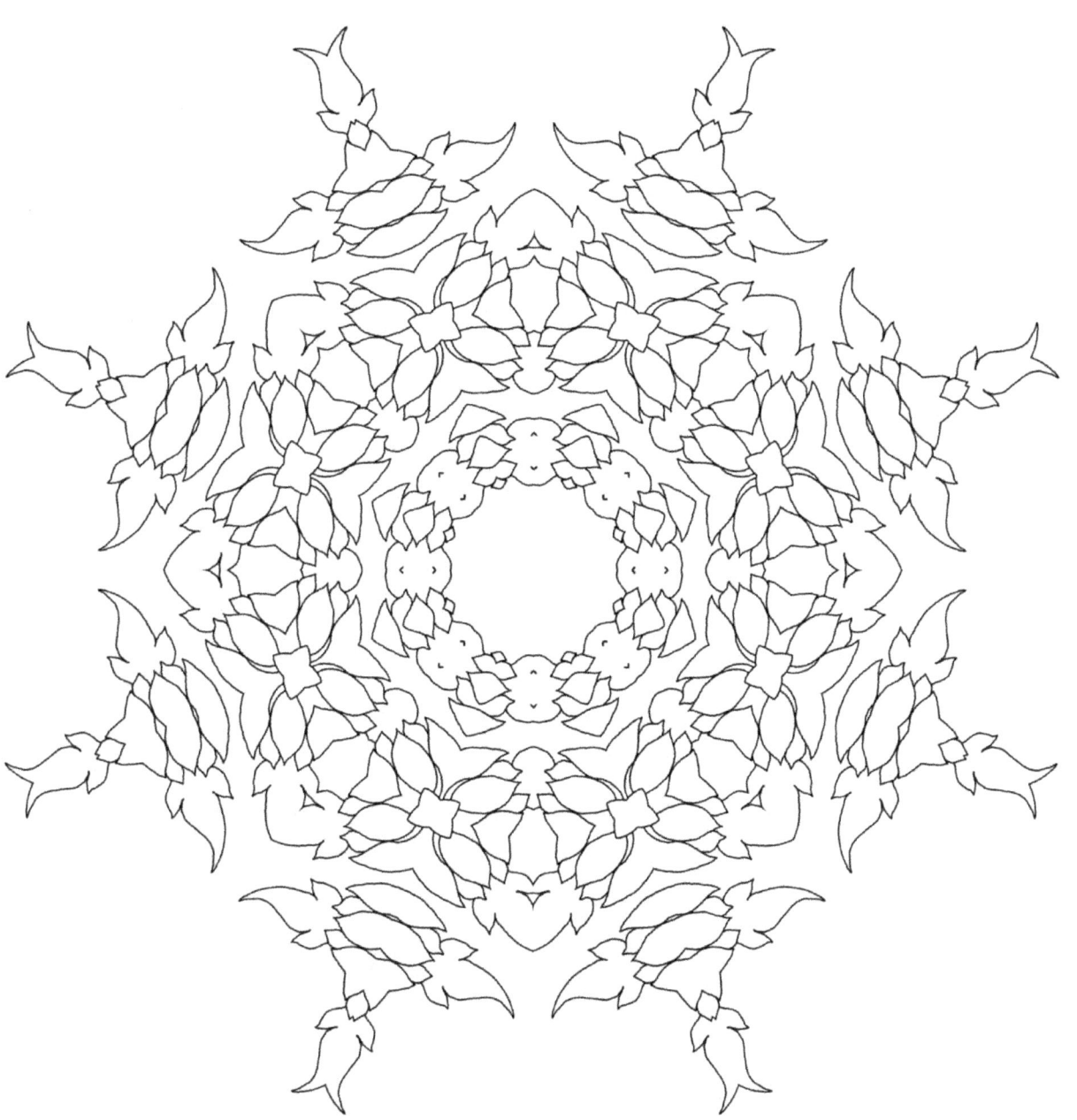

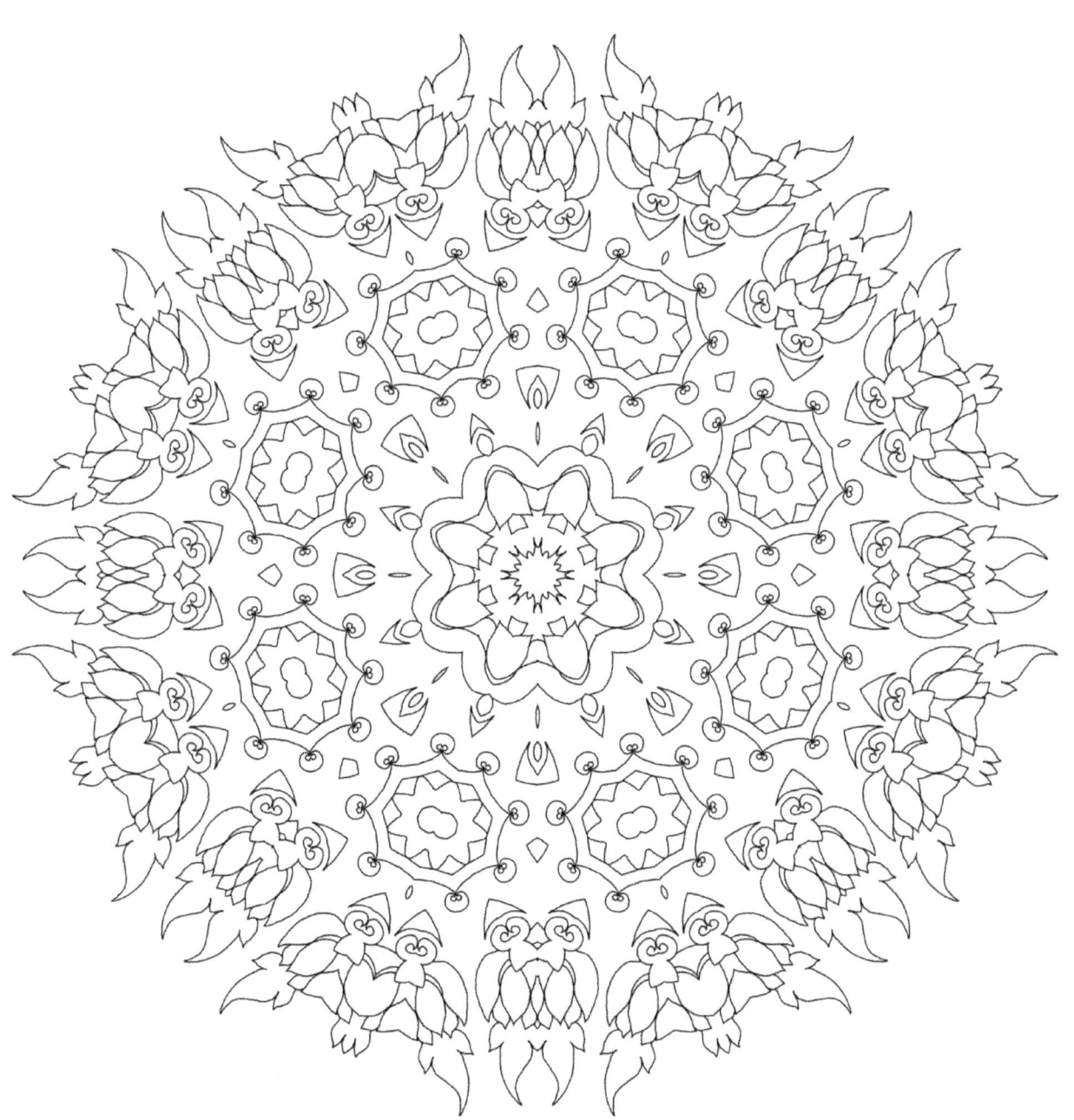

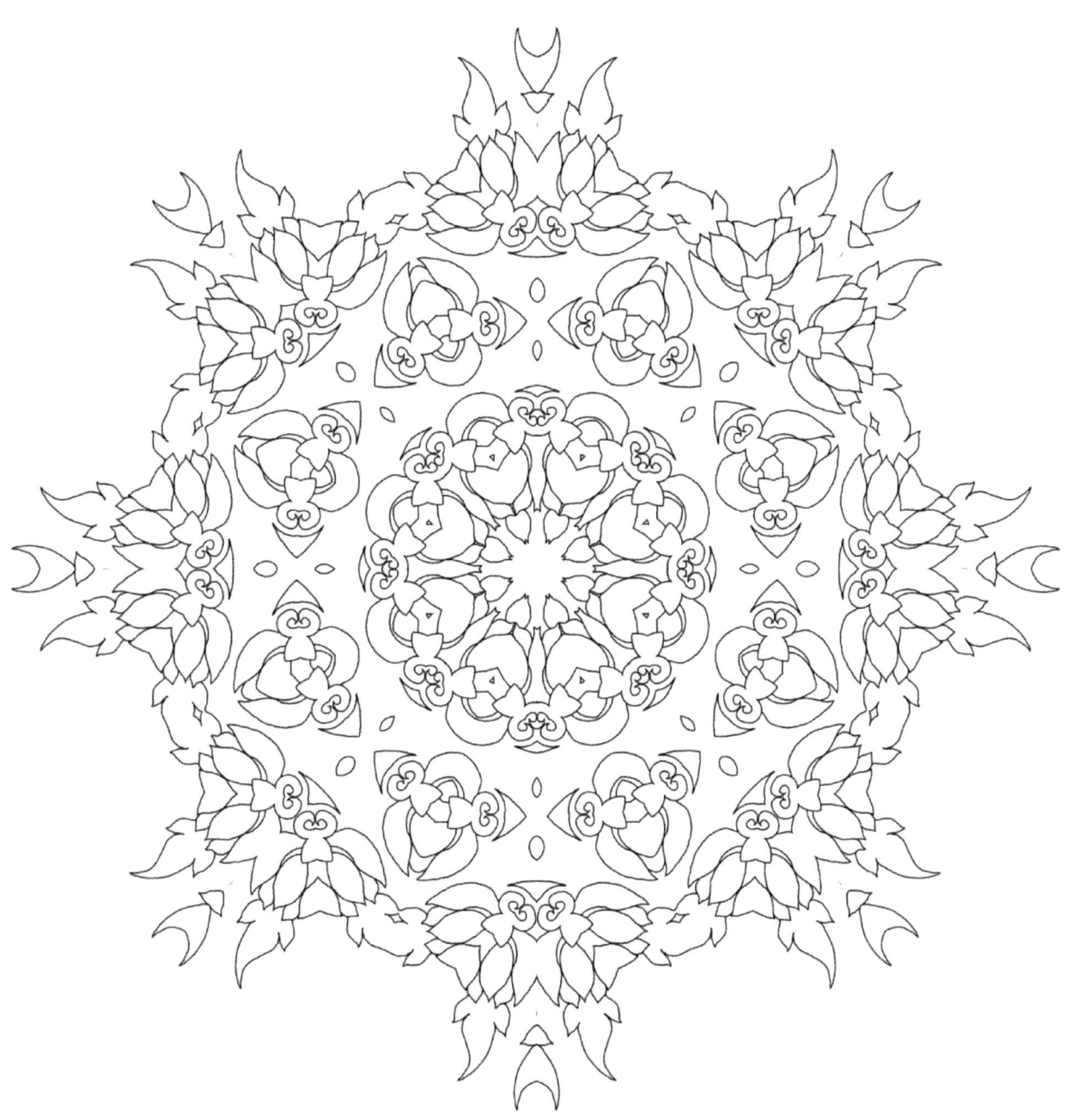

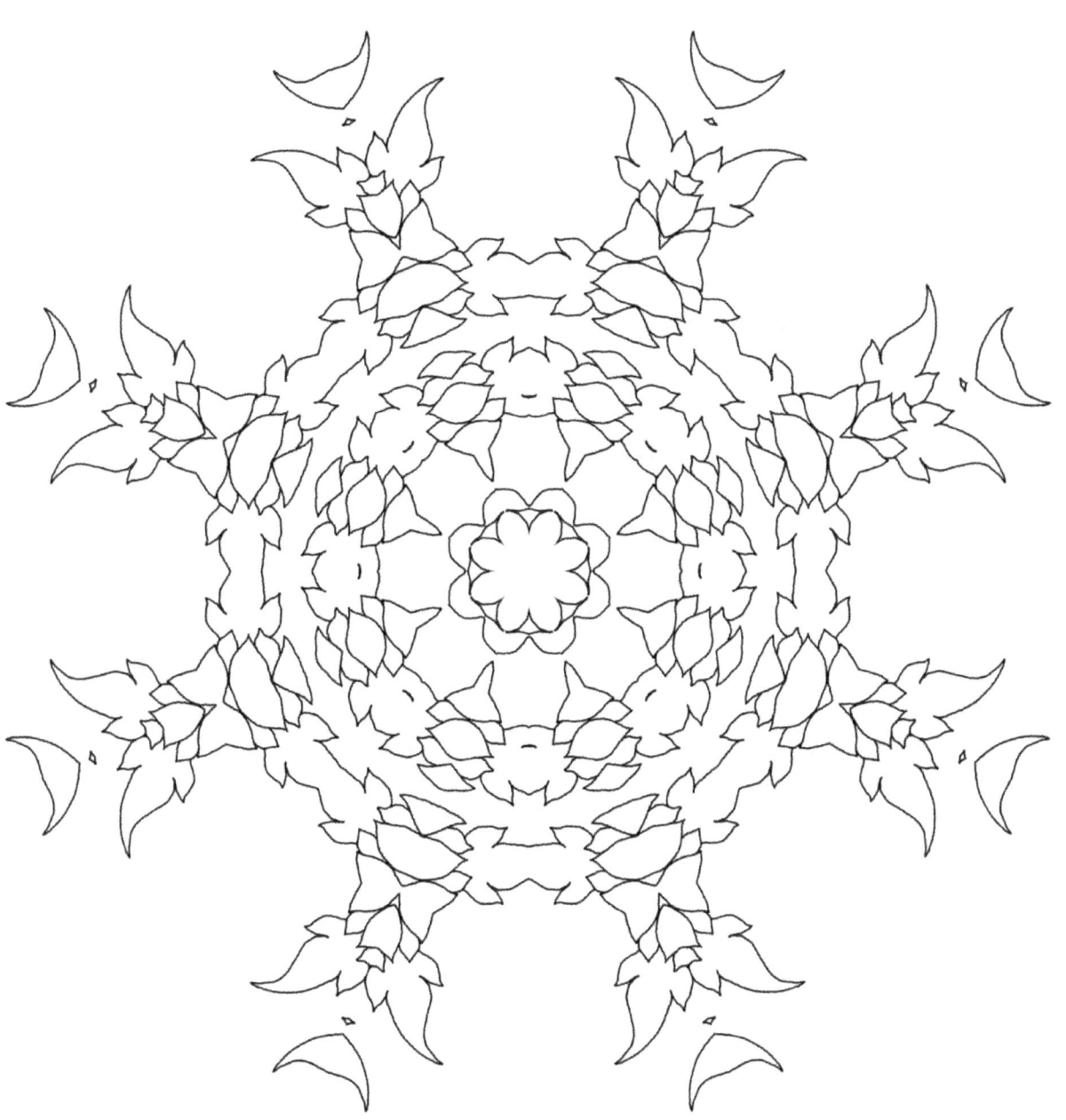

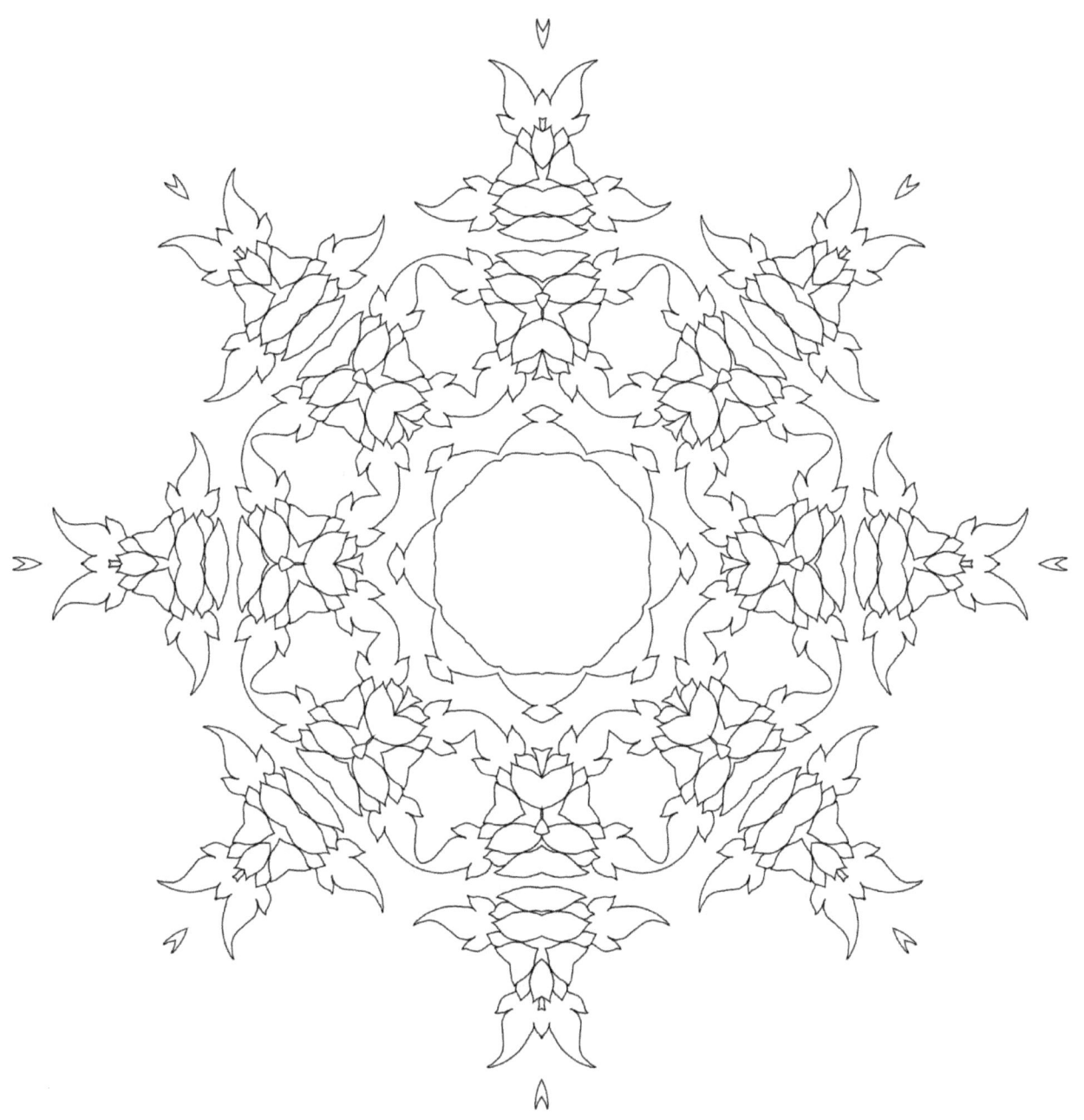

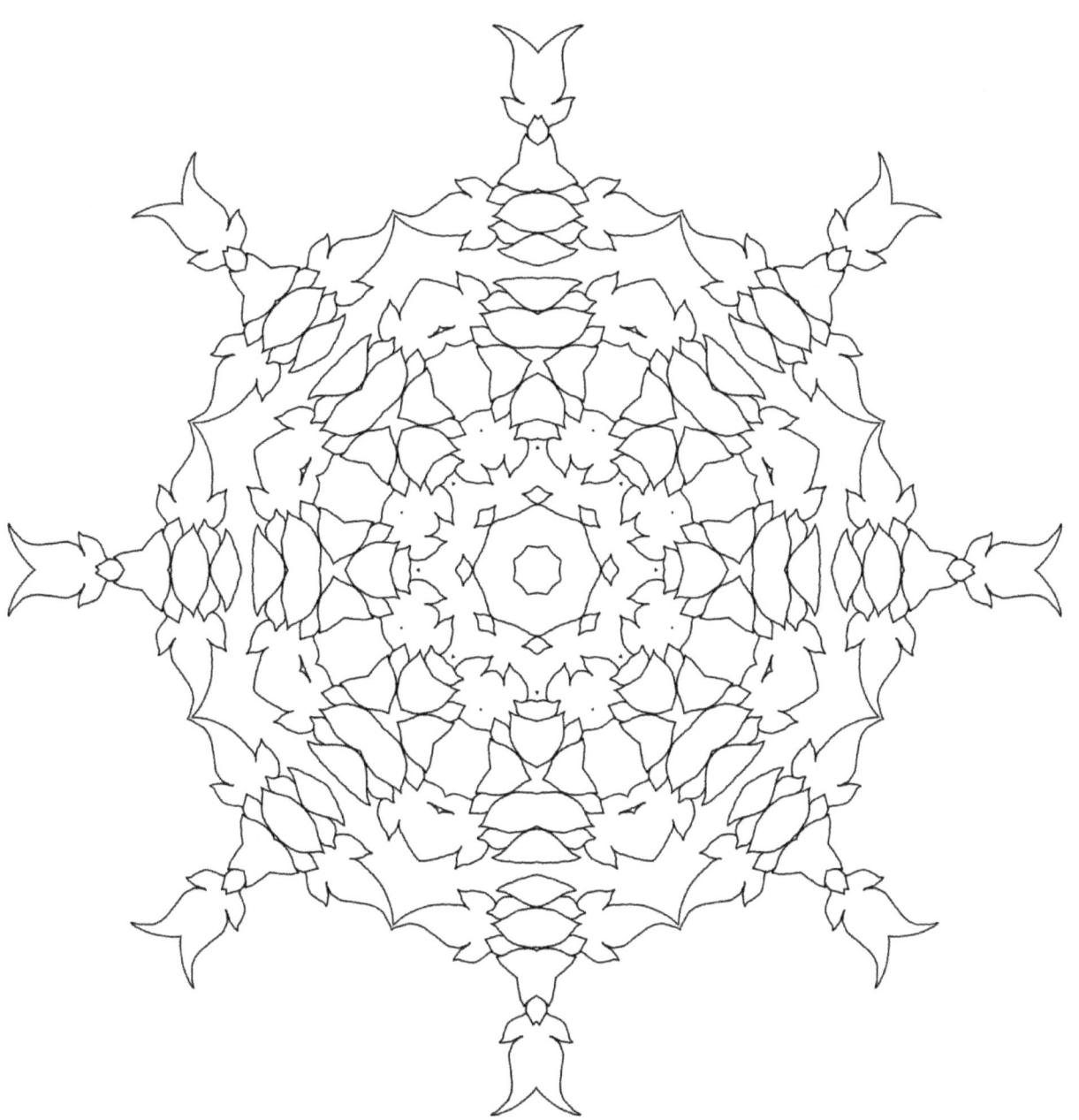

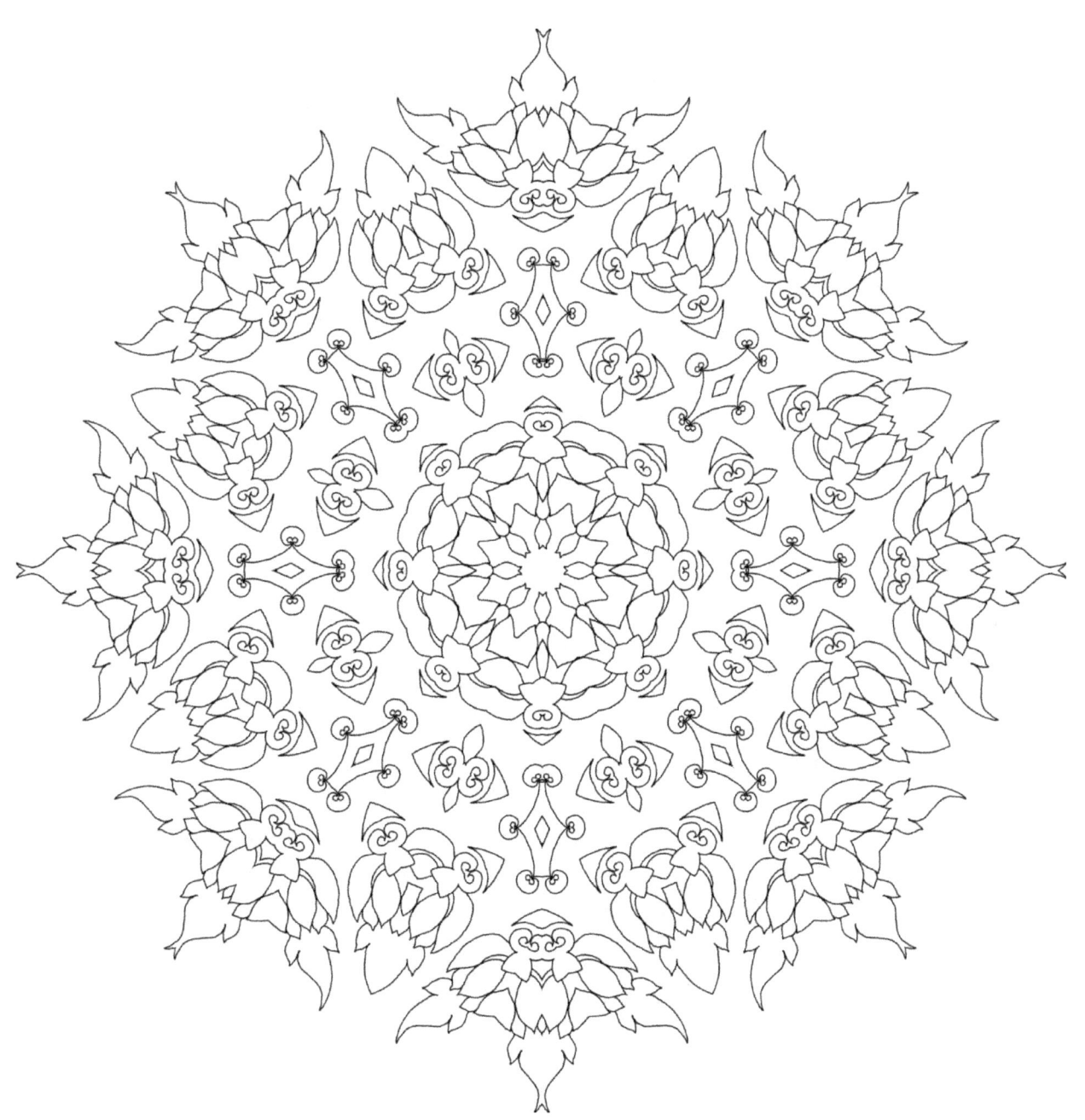

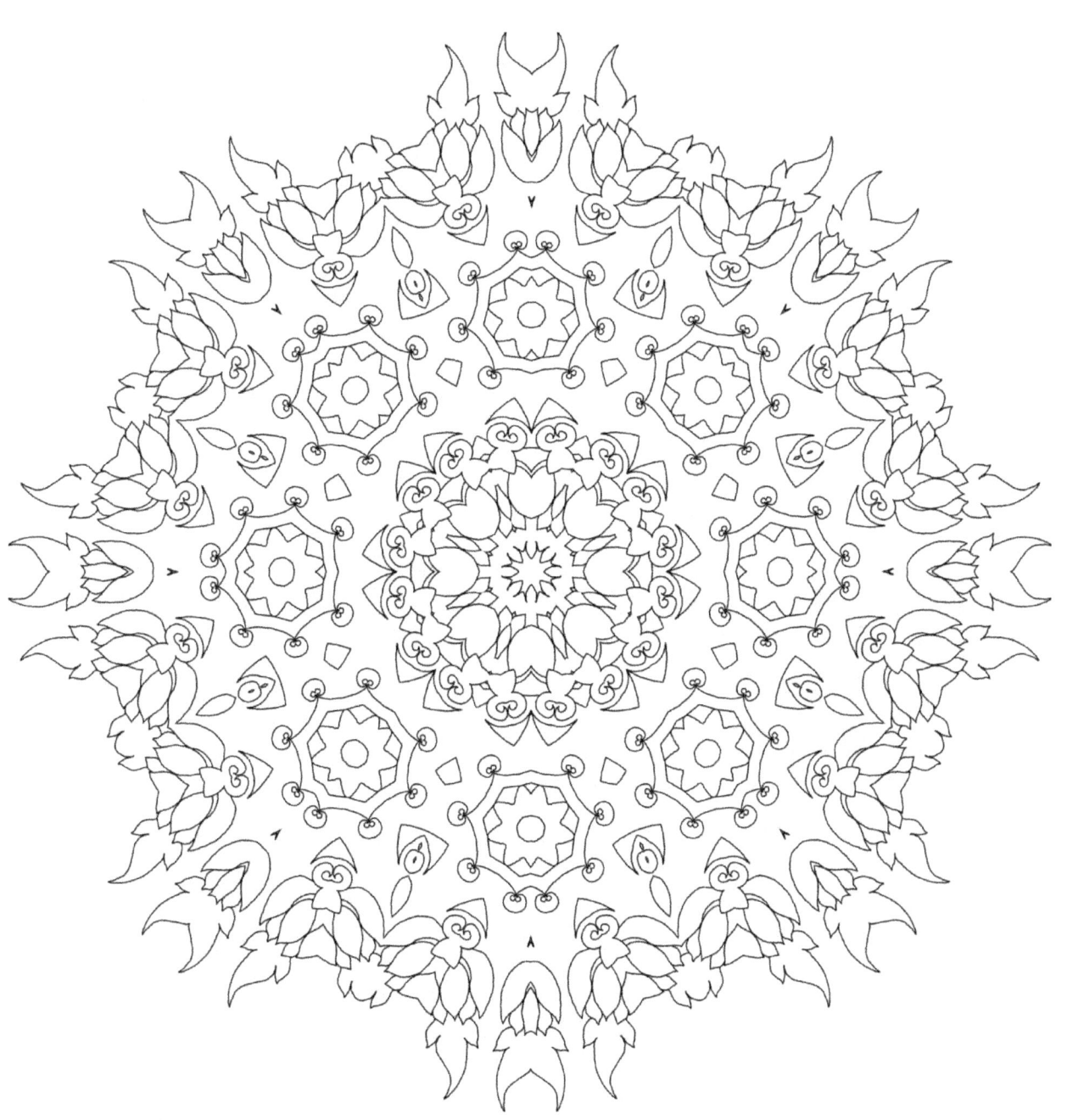

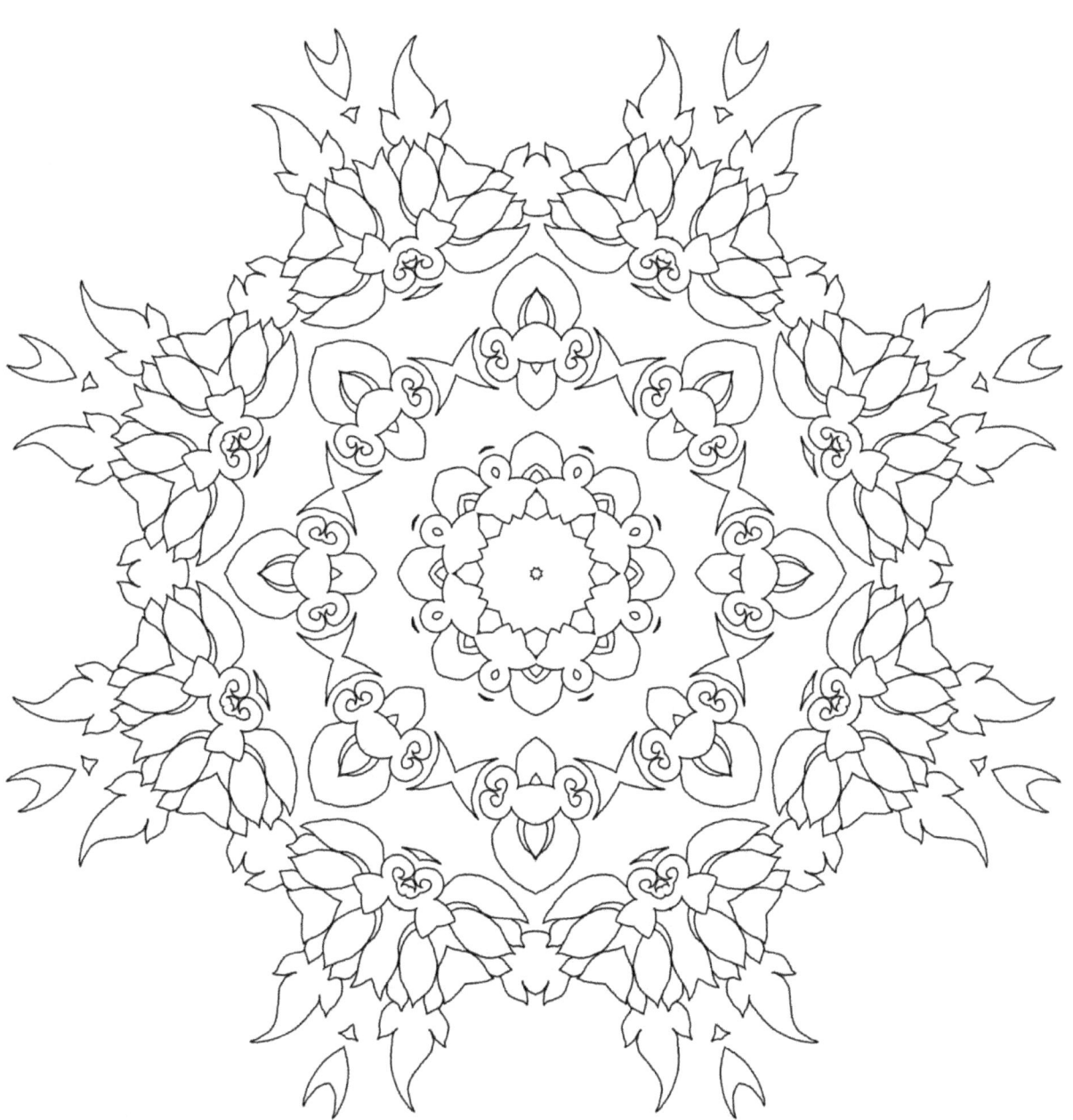

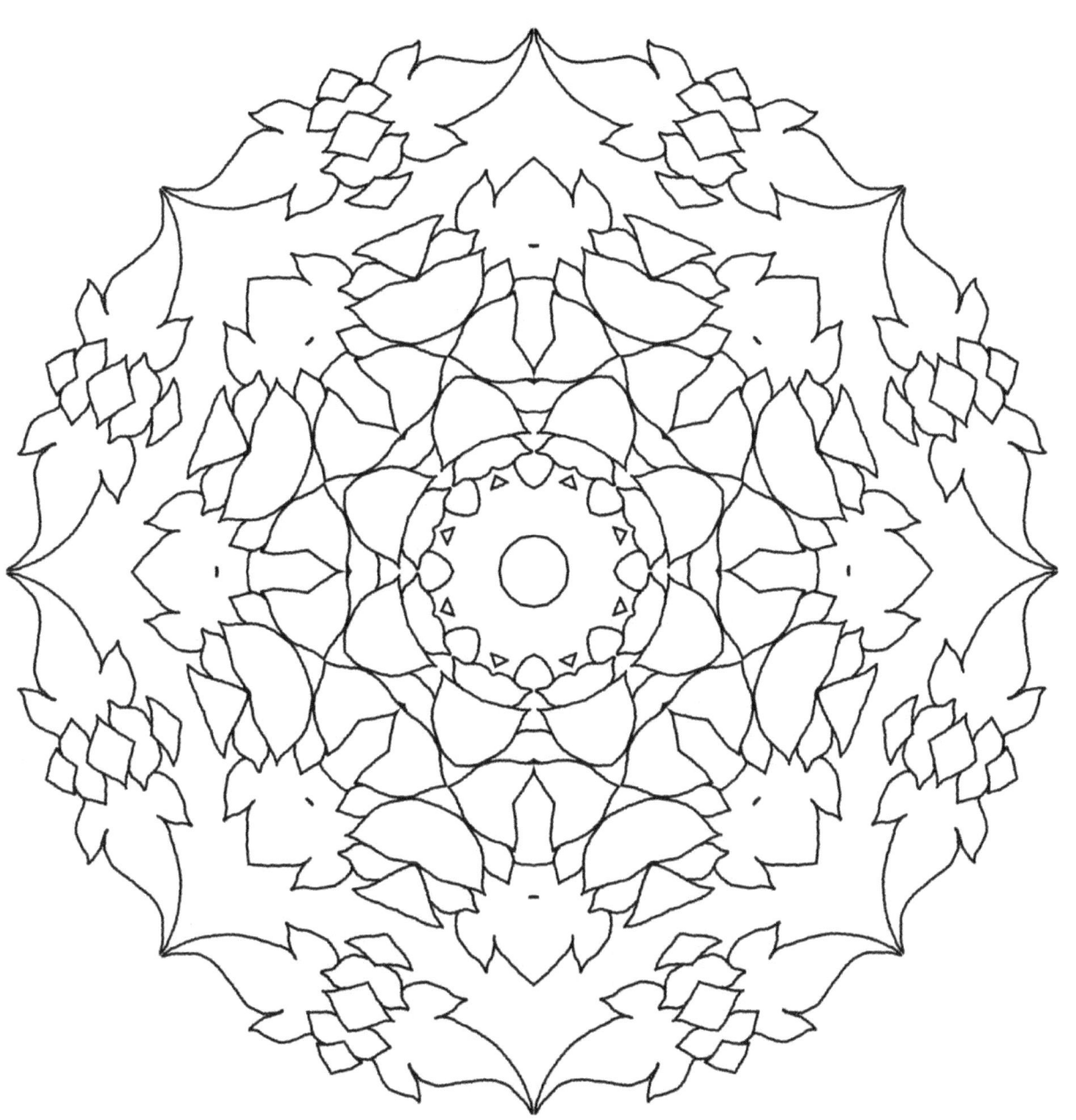

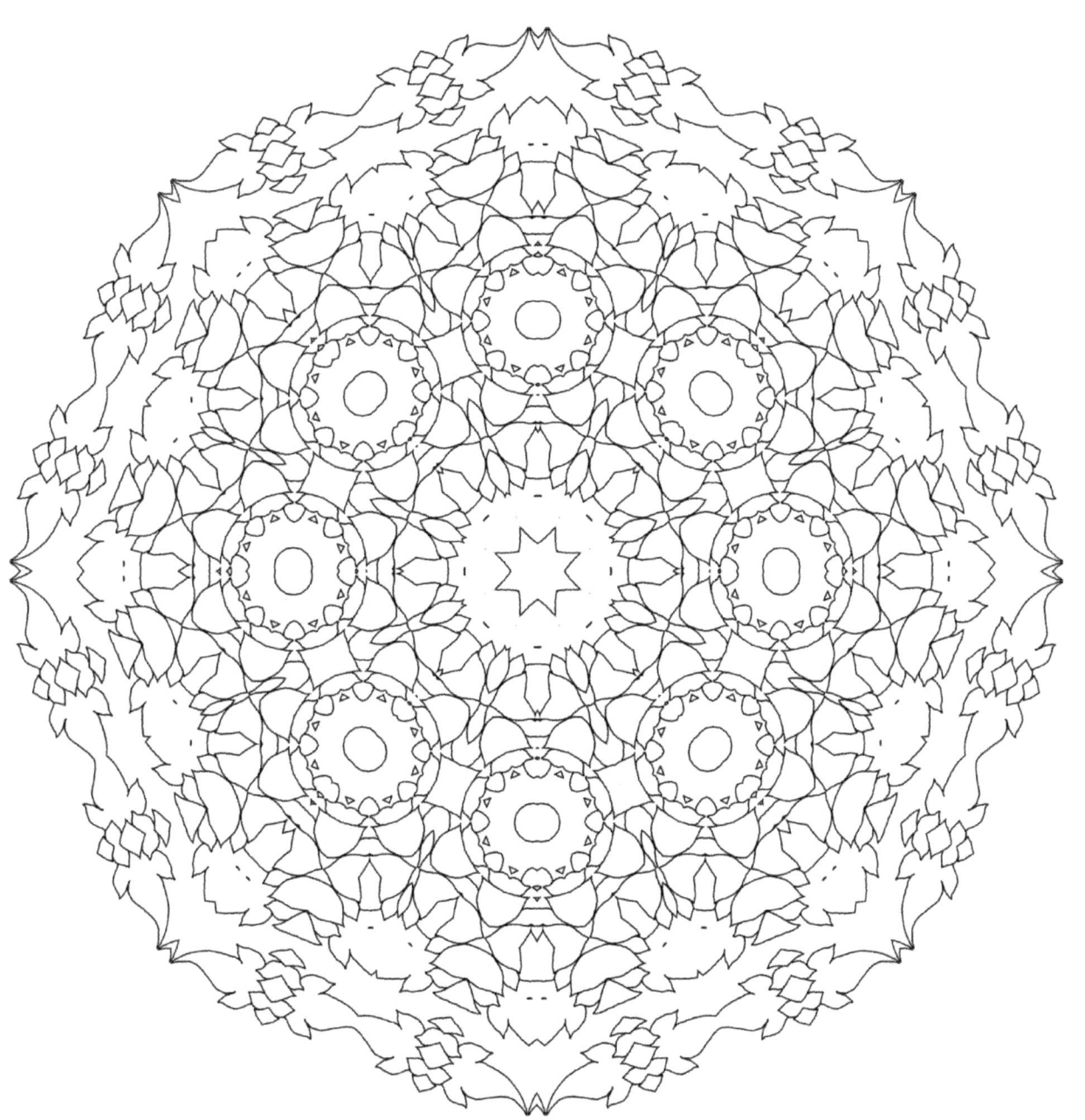

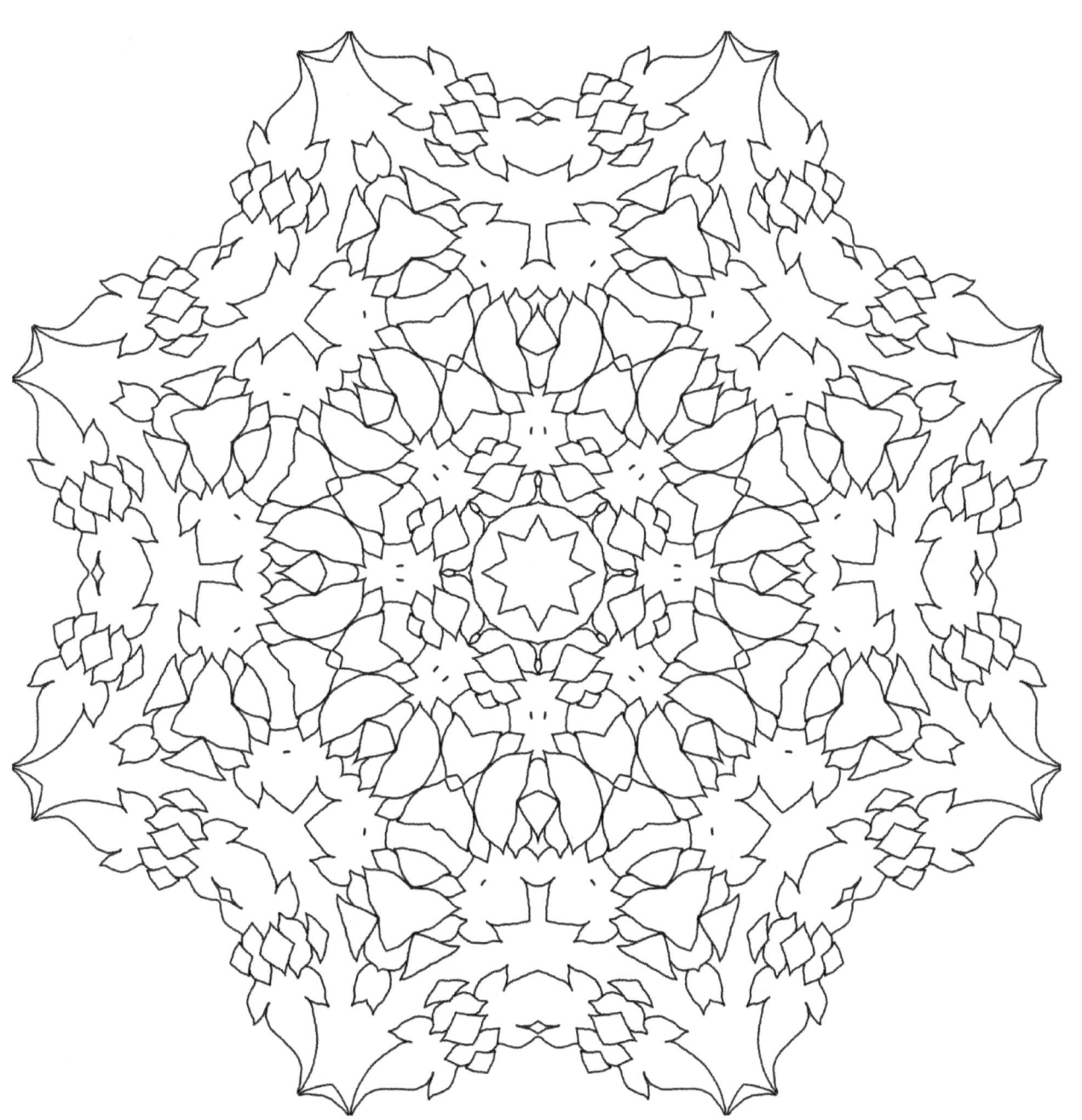

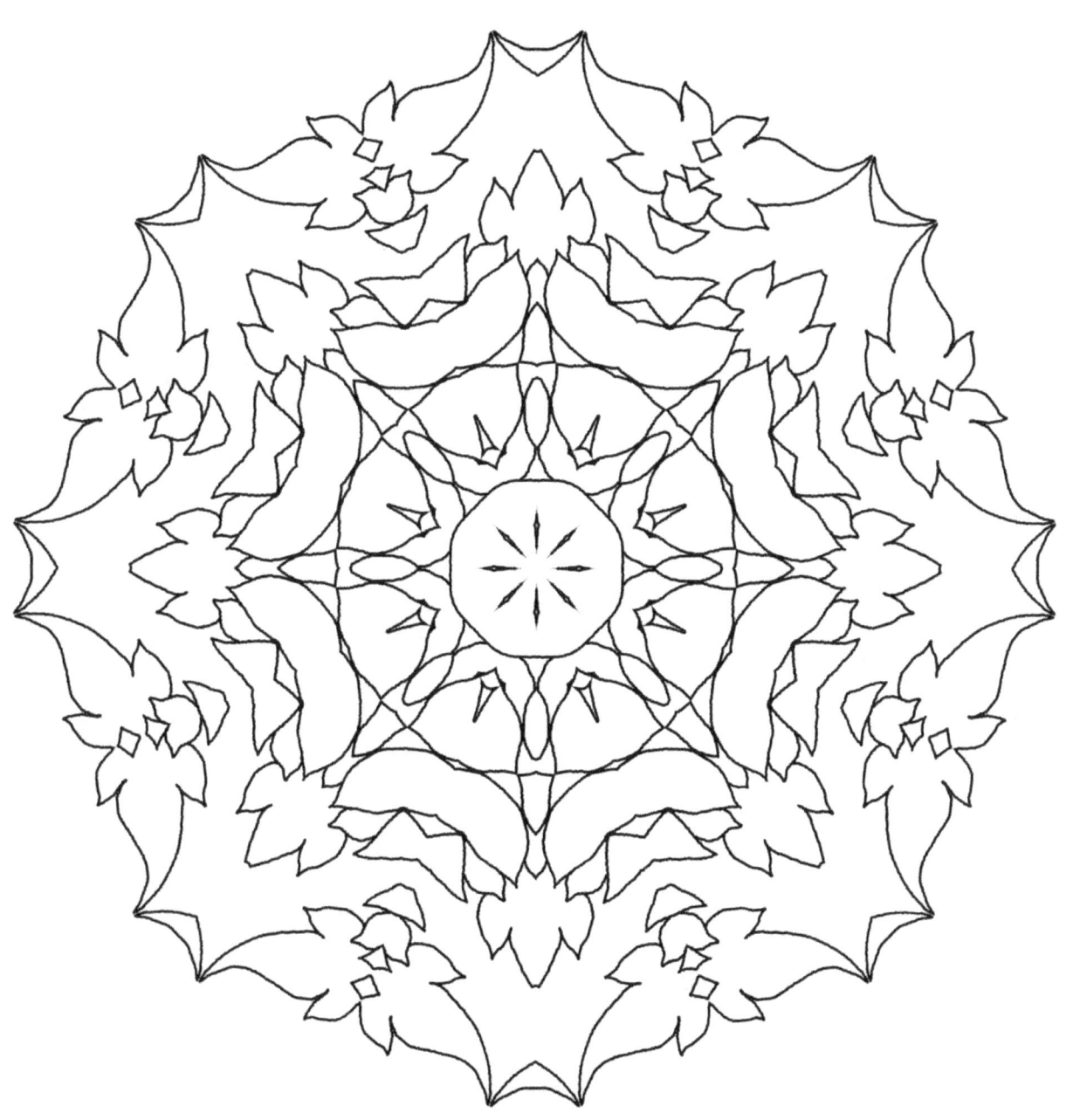

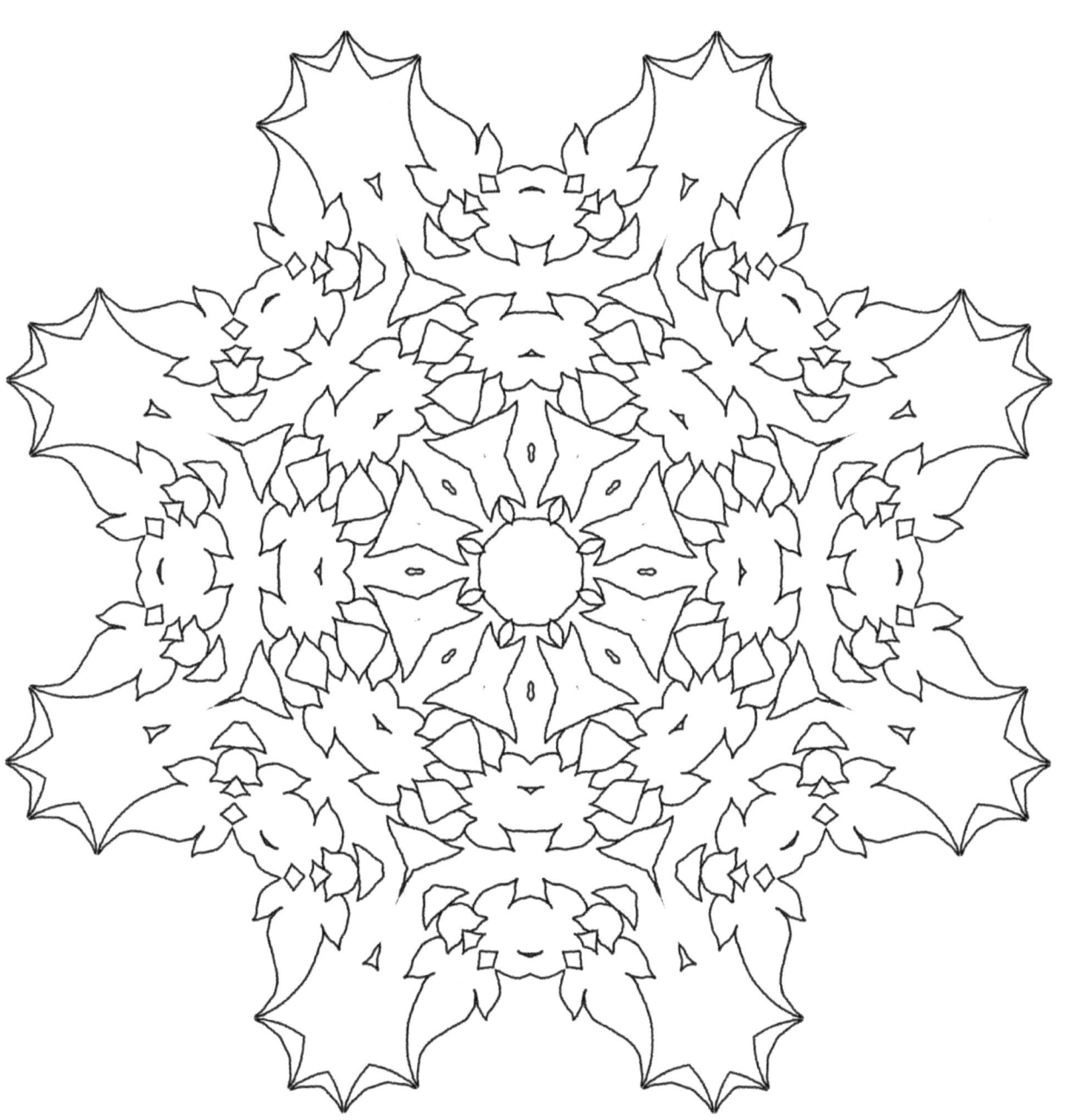

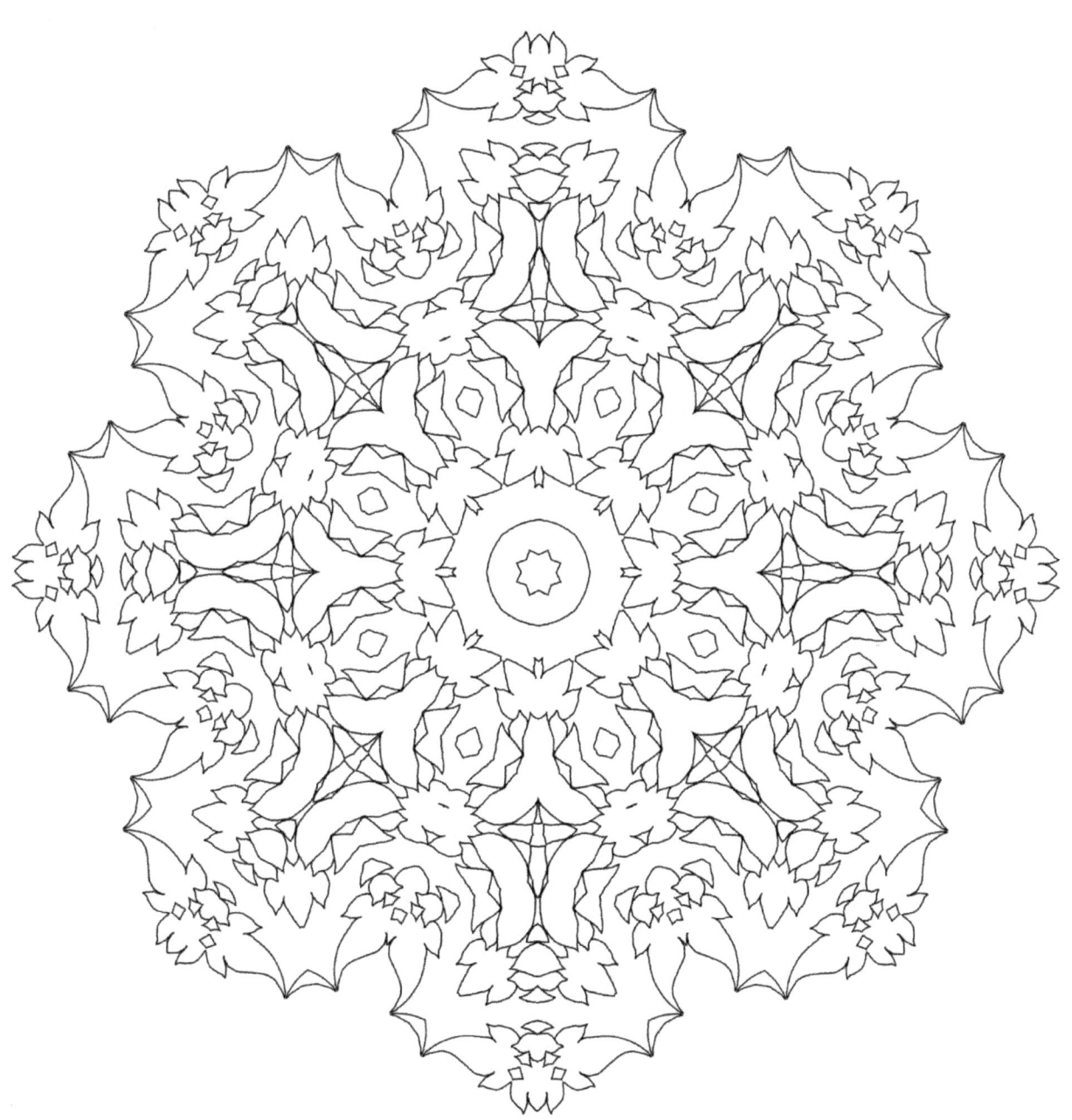

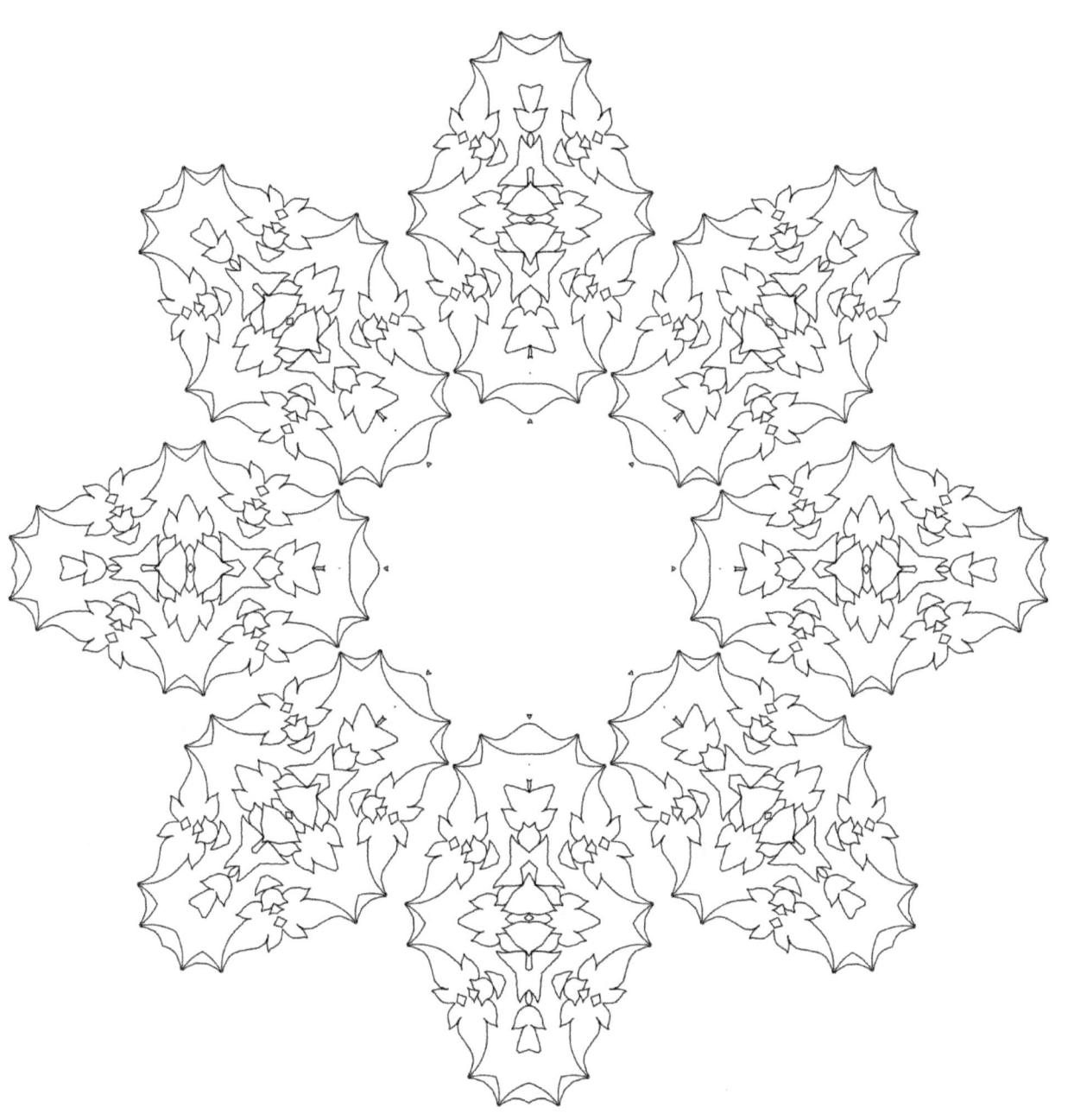

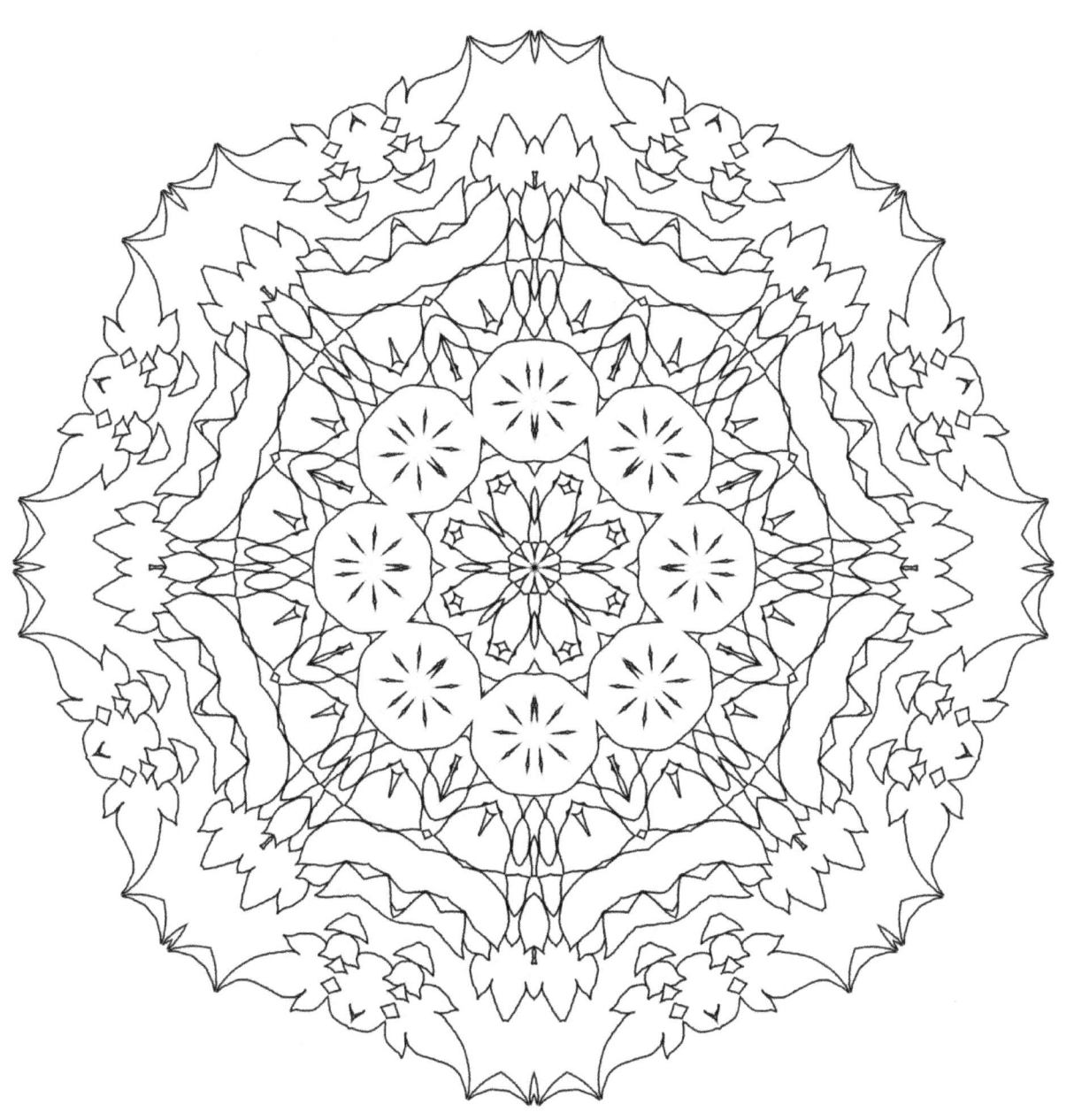

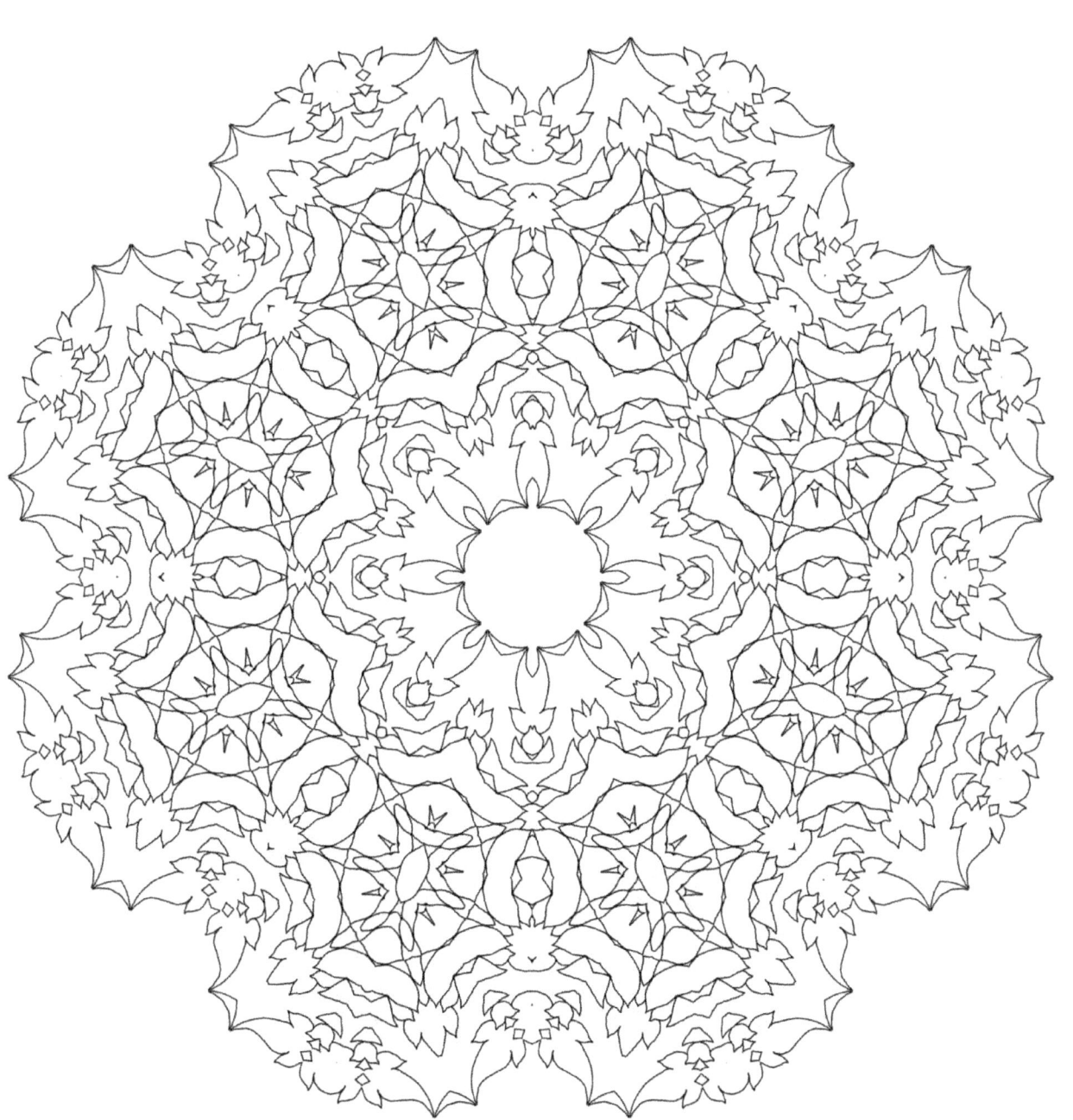

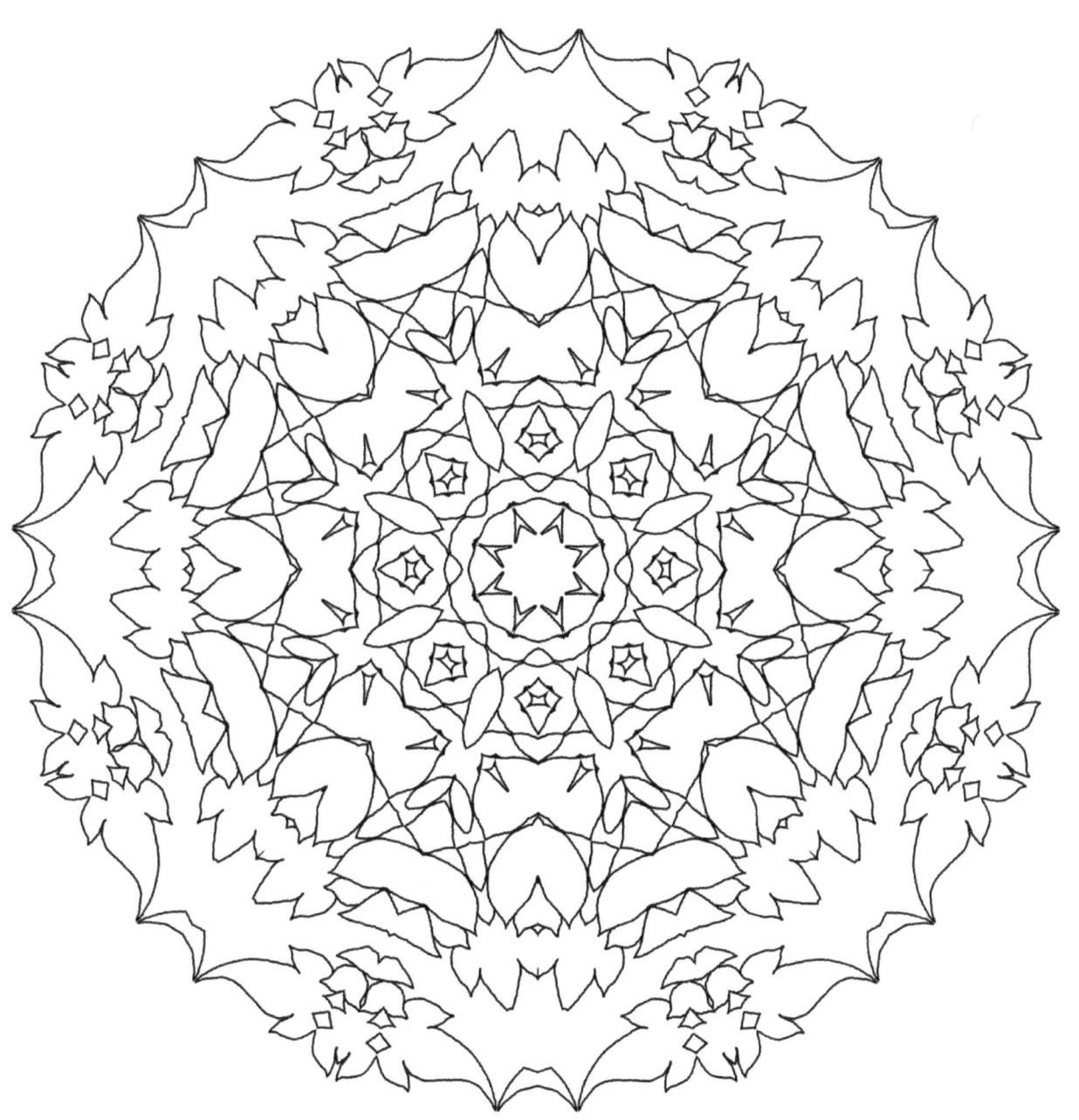

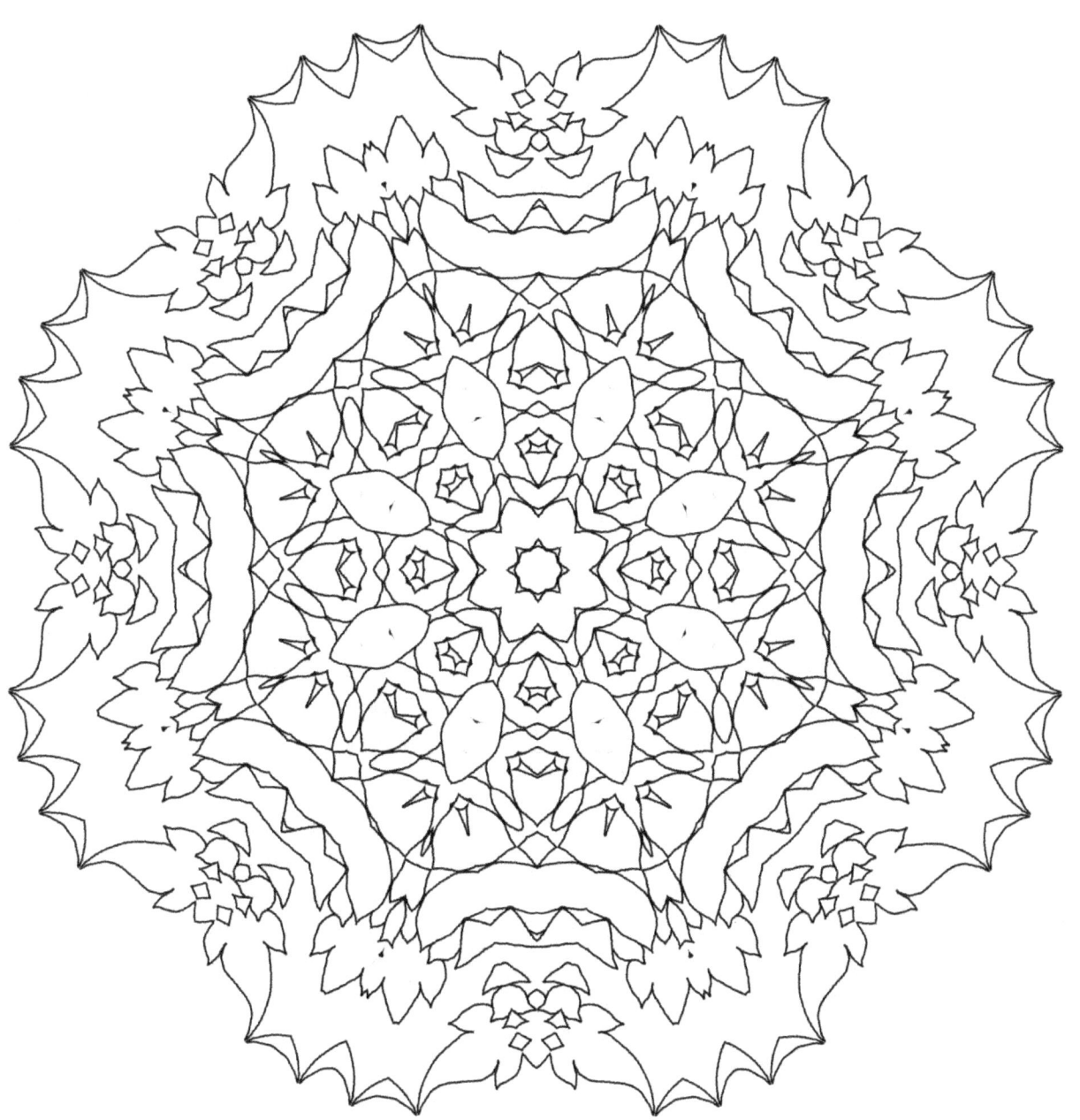

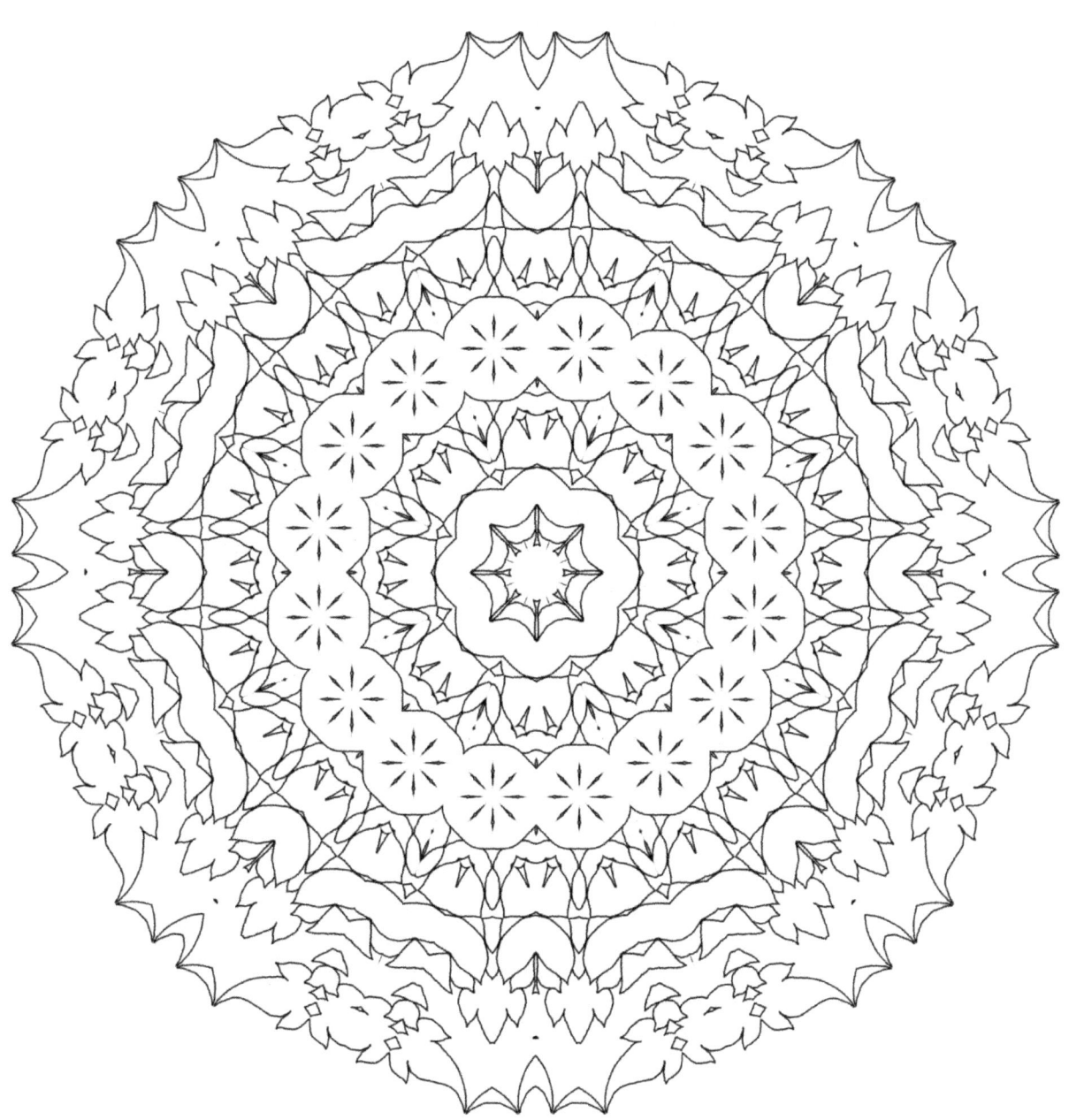

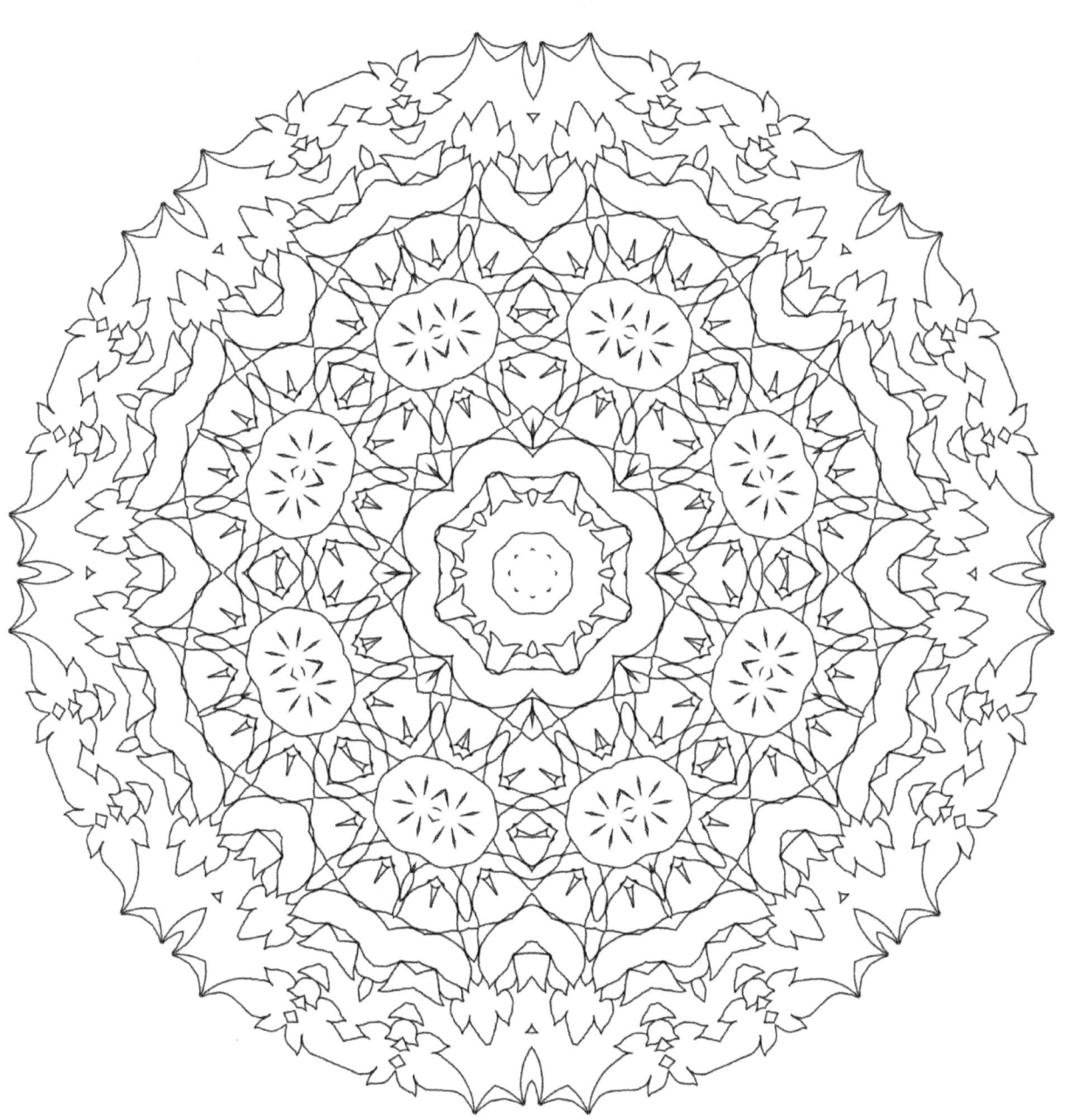

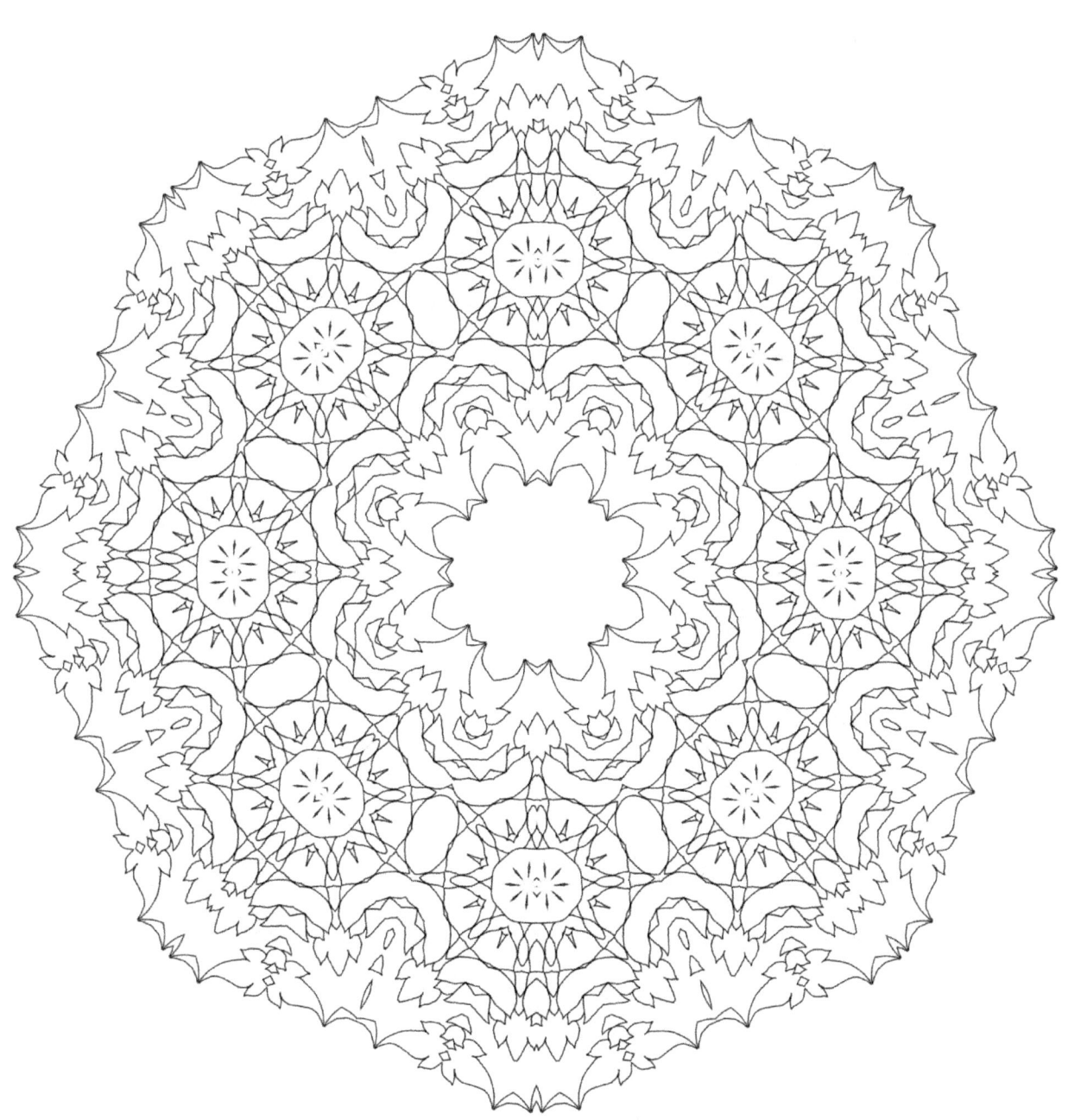

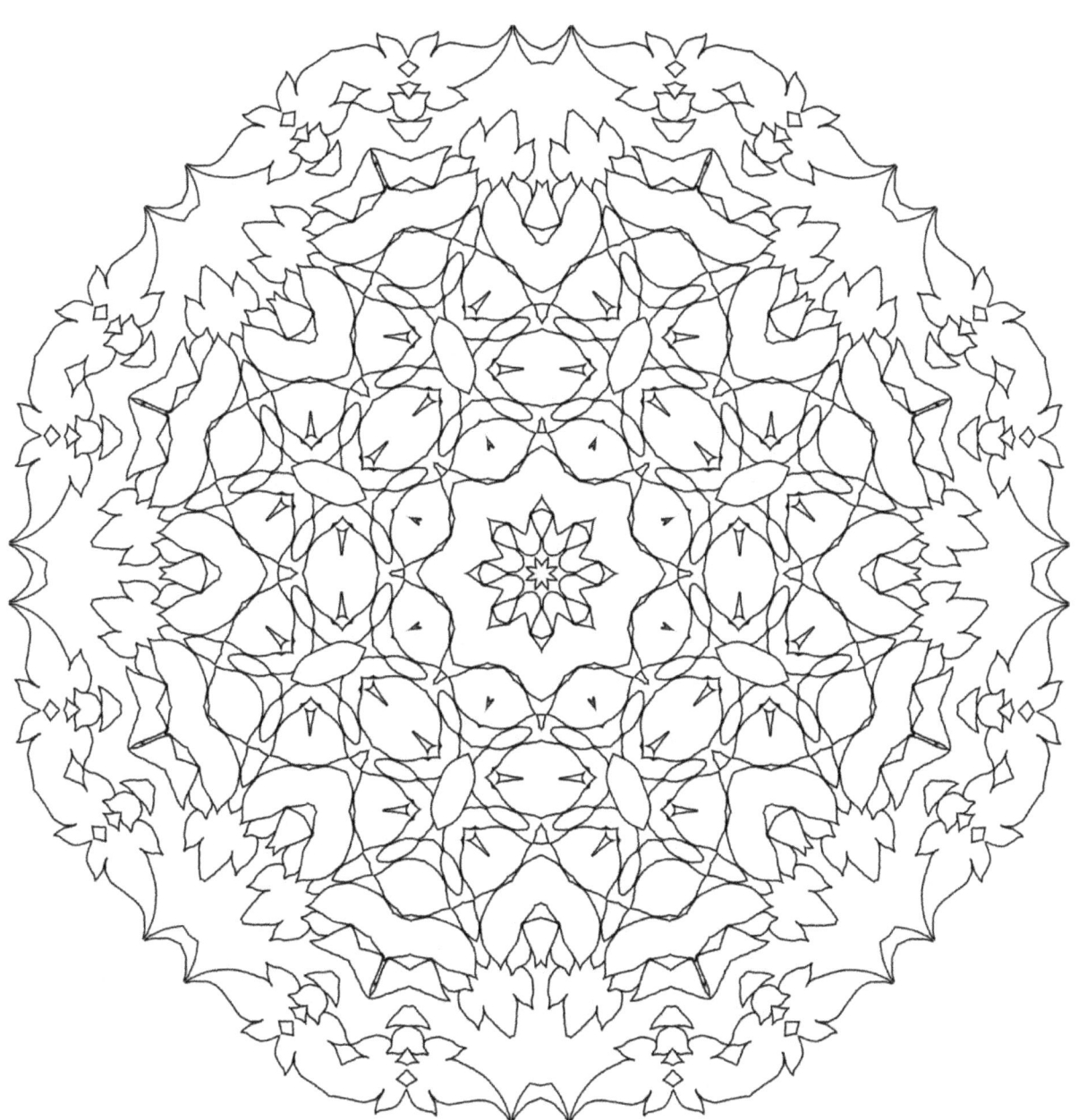

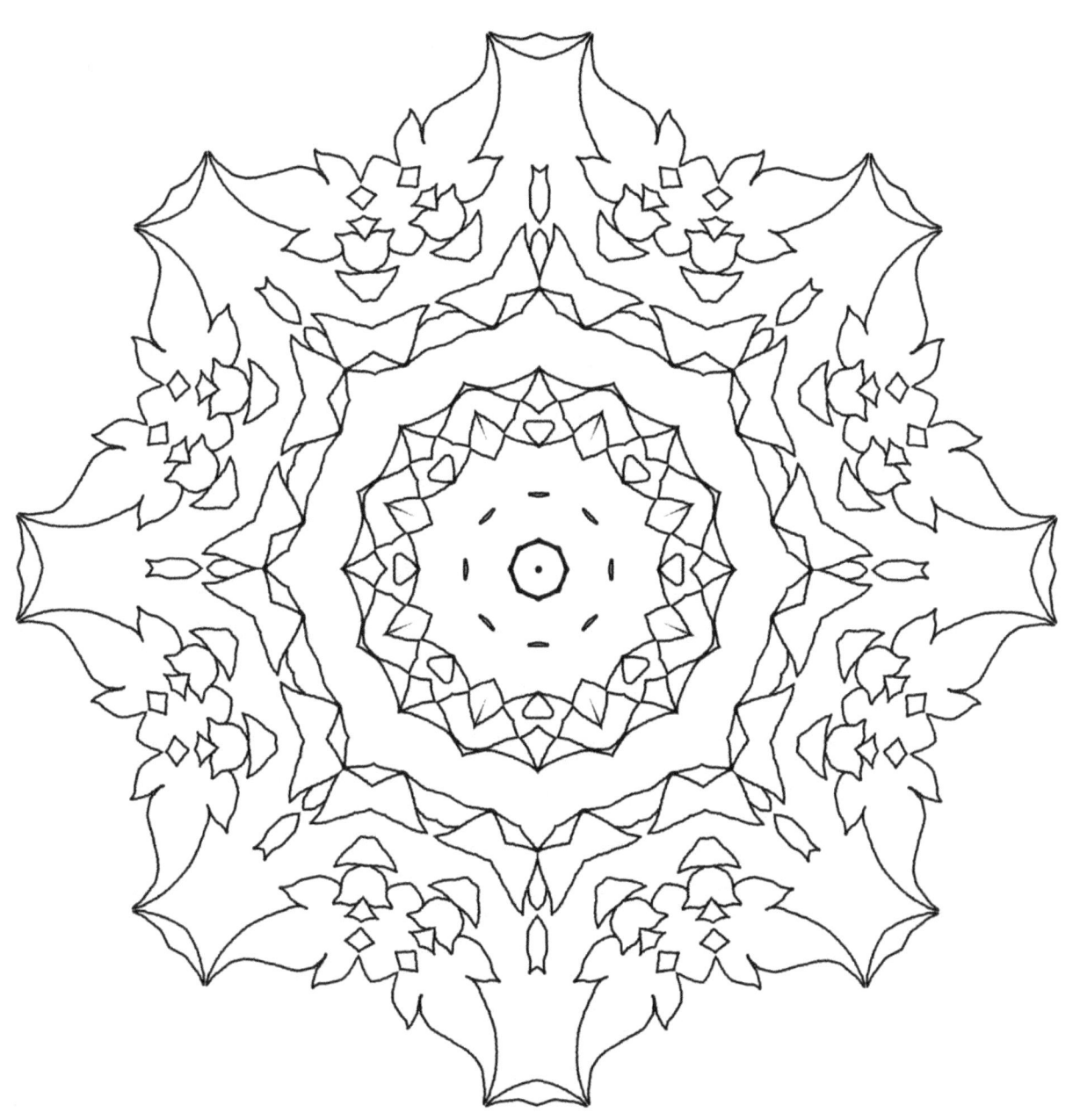

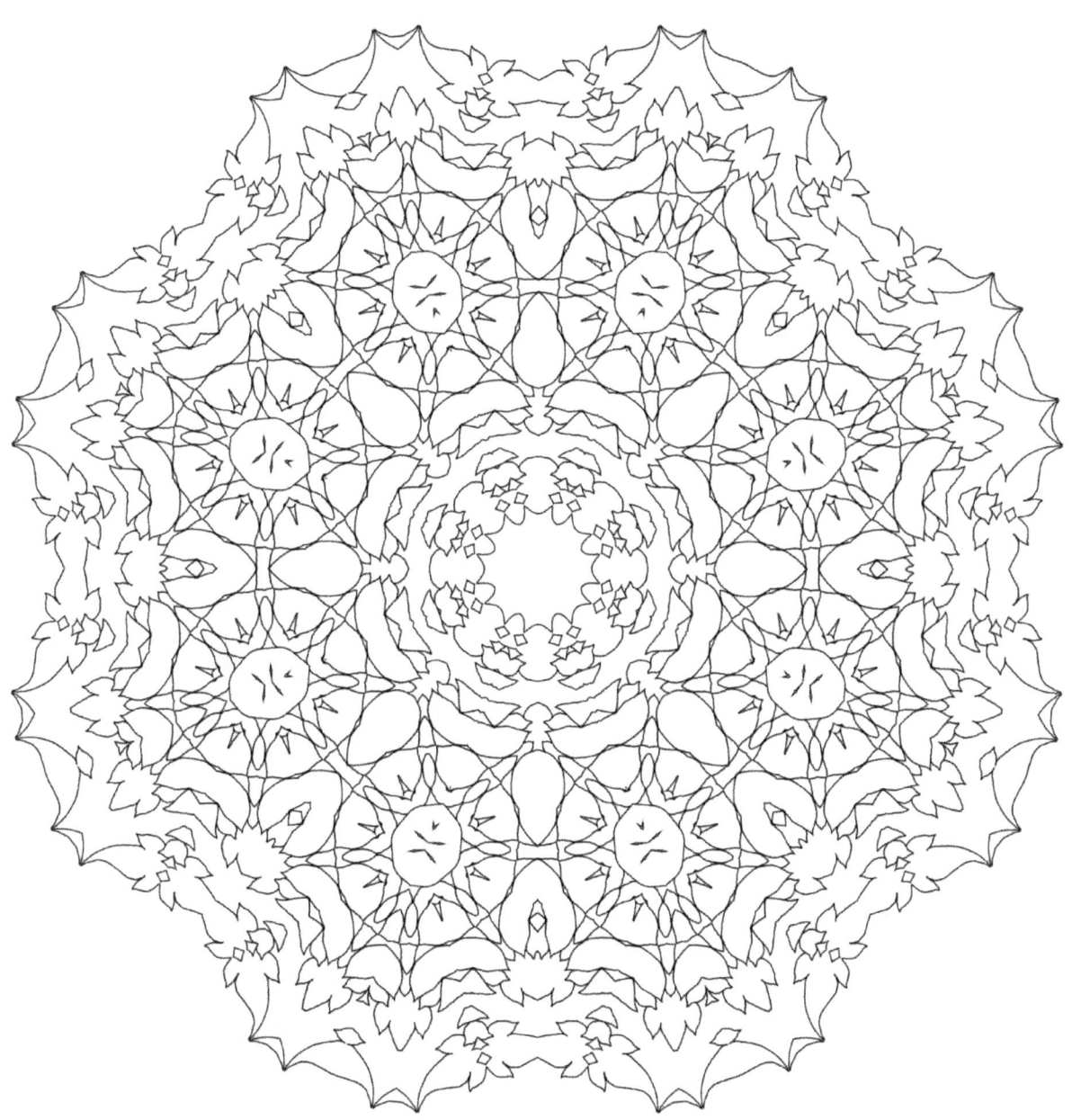

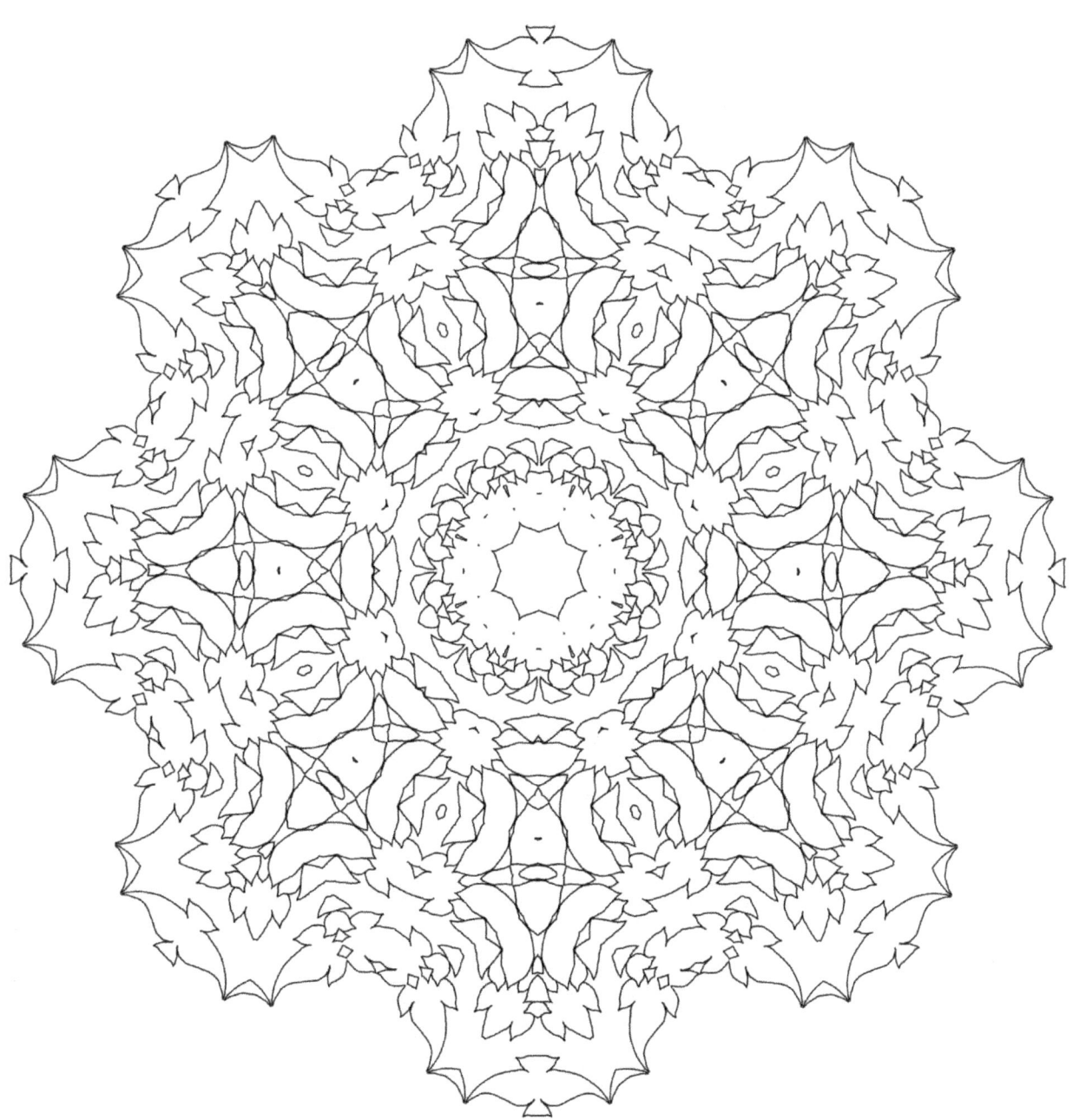

Thank you

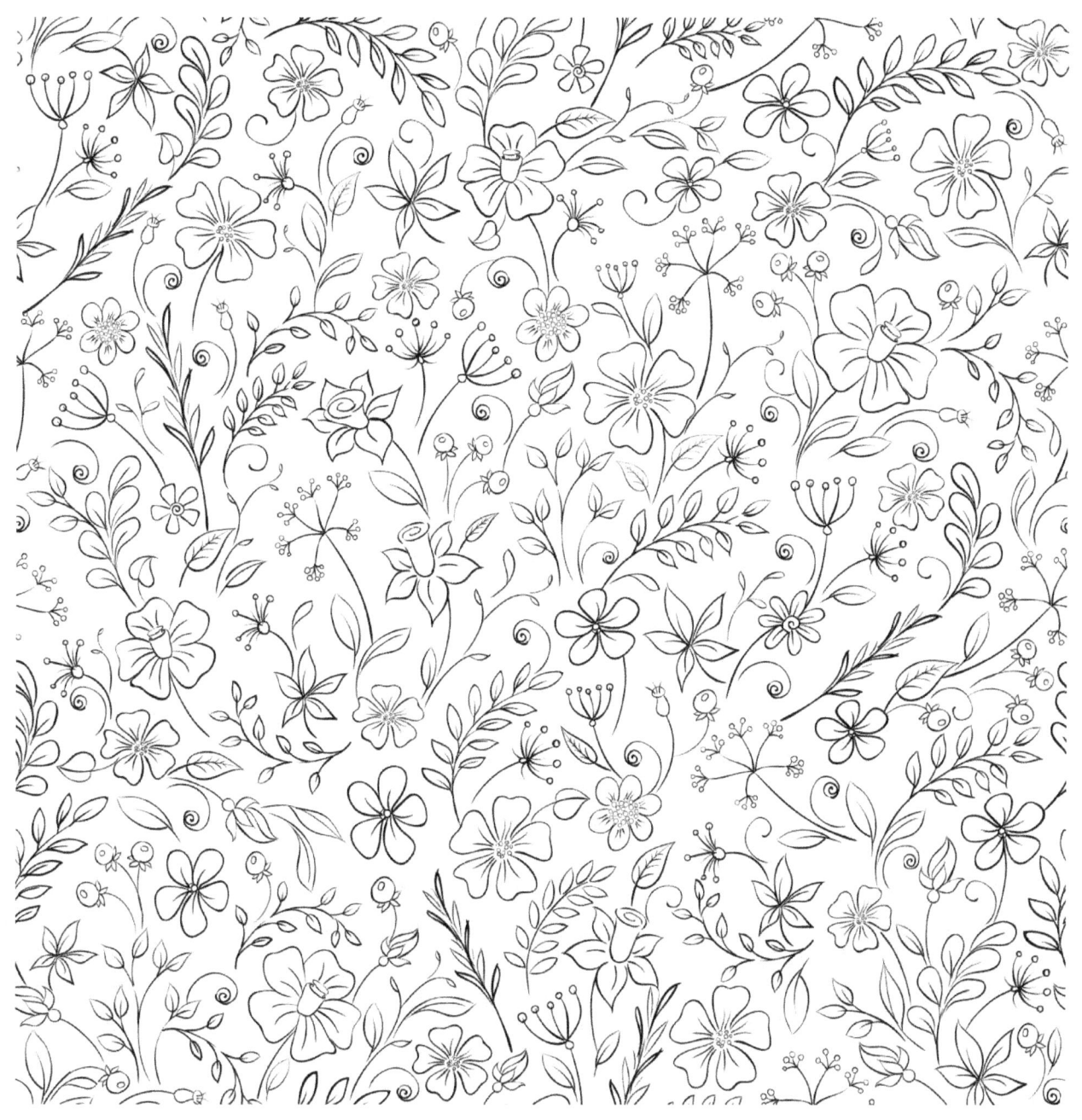

www.ingramcontent.com/pod-product-compliance
Lightning Source LLC
Chambersburg PA
CBHW081117180526
45170CB00008B/2890